LAUGHING

NORMAN N. HOLLAND

LAUGHING

A Psychology of Humor

CORNELL UNIVERSITY PRESS

Ithaca and London

First published 1982 by Cornell University Press.
Published in the United Kingdom by Cornell University Press Ltd.,
Ely House, 37 Dover Street, London W1X 4HQ.

International Standard Book Number 0-8014-1449-0
Library of Congress Catalog Card Number 82-7458

Printed in the United States of America

*Librarians: Library of Congress cataloguing information
appears on the last page of the book*

*The paper in this book is acid-free, and meets the guidelines
for permanence and durability of the Committee on Production
Guidelines for Book Longevity of the Council on Library Resources.*

To all the banterers, buffoons,
burlesquers, caricaturists,
cartoonists, clowns, comic or
comedians, cynics, funny friends,
gongorists, ironists, jesters and
jokers, laughing lovers,
mythmakers, parodists, punsters,
quipsters, raconteurs, railers,
satirists, scoffers, wits and
witlings, zanies, and one wise
wife who over the years have
made me laugh*

*But see p. 175.

Contents

Preface

She continued to laugh on some days, to cry on others,
unfolding the design of her identity.
—DENISE LEVERTOV

I like to laugh. I always have. I can remember listening as a
schoolboy to such long-gone radio comedians as Joe Penner
and Parkyakarkus, among the first in a line of comics that was
to extend through Fred Allen, Jack Benny, the brothers Marx,
Milton Berle, Sid Caesar and Imogene Coca, Mort Sahl, Ernie
Kovacs, "Laugh-In," Monty Python, Woody Allen, Mel Brooks,
Firesign Theatre, Robin Williams, SCTV, and who knows who
next? They are my tutelary spirits, paradigms for less showbiz
kinds of laughter: jokes around a circle of friends, banter at
work, the hilarity of a party, the joy of sex (*Enter laughing*),
the efforts and antics of my children, the strong, wise ironies of
one's aged relatives, and all the other levities that salt and
solace living.

Laughing is a labor of love—or laughter. I am returning to a
happy opportunity of more than a decade ago, when for half a
dozen years I had the good fortune to teach a course called (by
me) "The Comic Sensibility" or (by the students) "The Cosmic
Sensitivity." We studied jokes and cartoons and also the great
comic masterpieces: *Don Quixote, Tristram Shandy, The Canter-
bury Tales*, the *Decameron*; films by Bergman, Fellini, and Chaplin; opera by Gilbert and Sullivan; plays by Aristophanes,
Molière, Chekhov, Shaw, and Shakespeare.

9

We asked such questions as Why do we laugh? Why does something subtle and complicated and mental lead to this spasm in cheeks and belly? What is the special pleasure of comedy and laughter? Why is a thing funny at some times but not at others? Why is something funny to one person but not to another? And on and on.

These questions lured me like a big-game hunter into the jungle of psychology, where I bagged great hulking psycho-analytic theories about responses to literature and published them as *The Dynamics of Literary Response, Poems in Persons,* and *5 Readers Reading.* But what have I done about laughter, the most immediate of literary responses?

Laughing marks a return to that earlier, cozier inquiry, but it is also a personal test: Can I apply what I think I have learned in these intervening years to what led me to ask about response in the first place—laughter? If I have learned something about literary and other responses, can I say something to you about humor worth adding to the volumes already offered by the hundreds of theorists and psychologists who have already studied laughing? These are my own highly personal questions about this book. Now your response to *Laughing* will make them not into answers, but into questions for you as well.

Laughing has two parts. First, an (I hope) exhaustive, perhaps exhausting, survey of existing theories about the comic. I think you may feel, as I do, that precisely because there are so many theories and pseudotheories as to why we laugh, they tend to cancel one another out, leaving the question unanswered. But . . .

The second half of the book reports on some real people laughing, one person especially, leading to an ambitious an-swer to "Why do we laugh?" which leads to some questions that unsettle that answer. The questions, in turn, make it pos-sible to understand the hundreds of traditional theories and variations on theories in a larger, psychological framework within which they can answer the question better.

This, then, is only partly a book that asks (and answers),

"Why do we laugh?" It also asks, "How can we ask, 'Why do we laugh?'" And answers. For it seems to me that "Why do we laugh," which joins a sharing "we" and a universal "laugh" to a highly personal and cultural "why," raises some fundamental issues about the way we humans explain ourselves to ourselves.

For the help they have given me on the first, survey half of the book and the bibliography, I am much obliged to John Stuart, David Cooper, Ellen Golub, Mary Childers, Janice Doane, Laura Keyes, Thomas Albert, and Patrick Hogan, recent graduate students in English at the State University of New York at Buffalo. For help with the second half of the book I owe a large debt to several pseudonymous students, especially "Ellen," who has graciously allowed me to tell in great detail the story of some of her laughings. Friends and colleagues—Paul Diesing, Diana Hume George, Patrick Hogan, Laura Keyes, Arthur Marotti, Joseph Masling, Robert Rogers, Murray Schwartz, and David Willbern—have read various versions of the book and offered many suggestions for improvement. I hope I have succeeded in living up to their standards and kindness.

For the preparation of the manuscript, I thank Joan Cipperman for her efficiency and wit and Geri de Santis for her skillful work with HAL and the Electric Pencil. I am much indebted to Patricia Berens of the Sterling Lord Agency for placing the manuscript and to Kenneth Heuer of Cornell University Press for confident and helpful suggestions at a critical moment. I am grateful to Mrs. James Thurber and to B. Kliban and Workman Publishing for permission to reprint cartoons and to Barbara H. Salazar for her thorough and thoughtful copy editing. The acknowledgment of my greatest debt is tucked away in the dedication.

NORMAN N. HOLLAND

Amherst, New York

I WHY DO WE LAUGH?

1 *The Comic*

We don't understand it, and we don't quite trust it. Those are for me the two most immediate and obvious facts about the comic.

The comic is hard to understand because it alone, among the arts, has a specific physical reflex associated with it—laughter. We decide something is funny or not by whether we feel like laughing at it, even though we may not laugh out loud. The impulse physically to laugh remains the test. And laughter we distrust. "Having mentioned laughing, I must particularly warn you against it," wrote Lord Chesterfield to his son in 1748, "and I could heartily wish that you may often be seen to smile, but never heard to laugh while you live. Frequent and loud laughter is the characteristic of folly and ill manners. . . . In my mind, there is nothing so illiberal and so ill-bred as audible laughter."[1] Earlier in that decorous century the essayist Joseph Addison recalled a Capuchin monk who believed "that Laughter was the effect of Original Sin, and that Adam could not laugh before the Fall." In ancient times Ecclesiastes had written, "I said of laughter, It is mad. And of mirth, What doeth it?" Even the pagan philosophers before Socrates said that joking was inconsistent with pity—and preferred pity.[2] Neither the earliest preclassical writers nor their neoclassical descendants approved of laughing, yet all these ancients, I have no doubt, guffawed like the rest of us.

To be sure, the comic is by no means all laughable or funny

or, to use a useful synonym from the Greek, gelastic (pro-
nounced like a combination of jelly and elastic). It comes from
gelan, to laugh, a word that imitated the clucking of a (Greek)
chicken—more distrust and disparagement of laughter. We
gelasticists include in the comic not just the laughable, but
almost anything that has a nonpainful outcome, any "serious"
play with a happy ending, such as a soap opera in which
everything comes out all right, no matter how teary it was in
the middle installments. The funny is but one subspecies of the
comic.

Laughter may not define the comic arts, but it hovers in their
vicinity, giving a physical aura to the comic enterprise. We can,
after all, cause laughter purely physiologically, as by tickling or
the dentist's laughing gas, nitrous oxide. Babies and young
children laugh a lot, but out of pleasure or joy, not at wit.
They don't understand jokes. They don't laugh when adults
do. They don't, really, have a sense of humor. Laughter, the
funny, the comic all seem to occupy an anomalous psychosomatic space, somewhere between mind and body.

Laughter itself involves much more than an automatic physical response to a stimulus. Not all of us laugh at the same
things, nor are the same things always funny to the same person. Mostly, we laugh at a joke the first time only. A joke does
not usually make its teller laugh. Rather, the teller looks for a
second person to tell the joke to, and when that other person
laughs, the teller can laugh. If the other person doesn't laugh,
the jokester has "laid an egg" and (usually) feels deflated.

Some of the things we laugh at seem utterly inexplicable.
Consider Pascal's problem: "Two faces that are alike, although
neither of them excites laughter by itself, make us laugh when
together, on account of their likeness." Why do we find something funny in identical twins?

We simply don't know why people laugh. Not one theory of
the comic has won general acceptance. Despite that lack of
success, literary theorists and psychologists keep inventing
new theories, their futile efforts making yet another inexplica-
bly laughable gesture. As mine may, too.

We scarcely have a consistent attitude toward the comic (except distrust), let alone a theory about it. We "postmoderns" tend to regard the comic as less "serious" than the tragic (or, simply, things with unhappy endings). We inherit our attitude from the Romantics, who thought of comedy as primarily social and tragedy as primarily individual or cosmic. A Romantic aspires to a conflict between the individual and society. A Romantic prefers the isolated individual to the social, ritual, or conventional. For most intellectuals, alienation is a plus word. In classical and neoclassical times, however, when thinkers thought better of society and rituals, the comic and the tragic stood on a more or less equal footing.

In primitive times, the tragic did not exist at all. Our first drama was unequivocally comic. Yet, curiously enough, two thinkers as diverse as Karl Marx and Søren Kierkegaard agree that the comic is the last word. "The comic interpretation," Kierkegaard wrote, "is always the concluding one." And Marx: "The final phase of a world-historical form is its comedy." We find the comic most highly developed in the most sophisticated—even decadent—societies and individuals. In another sense, Kierkegaard's remark reminds me that it is possible to laugh even at serious things, but if you take the comic too seriously, you make yourself ridiculous.

Perhaps the comic seems less significant to us because it limits feeling, and in our post-Romantic era we value strong emotions, particularly sympathy. In Horace Walpole's famous epigram, "The world is a comedy to those that think, a tragedy to those that feel." We do not laugh, usually, at what we feel strongly about. A pratfall is funny, but not if it's taken by a dear friend with a bad heart.

We distinguish, therefore, between laughing *at* and laughing *with* someone, because laughter, by withholding pity, can serve as a weapon. We use it as a social corrective. We attack individuals, types, institutions, even deities by laughing at them. The comic does tend, therefore, to focus on realistic social situations—another reason it may seem less cosmic than the tragic. It also tends to deal with low people and to deal with people lowly, as mere bodies. Much of the comic relies on sexual and scatological jokes, while the tragic operates on a "higher" plane.

Very early in the game, Aristotle wrote the definitive theory of tragedy. It became definitive not because it settled our questions about the tragic forever and ever, but because so many people assumed that it did. When writers invented new kinds of tragedy, critics blithely redefined Aristotle to fit them. As a result, one needs very few terms to talk about the tragic, but the terms, such as "catharsis," "tragic flaw," and "recognition," can mean almost anything. I can scarcely think of a synonym for "tragic," yet I can scarcely define it, either.

The comic, however, lacks a theory everyone agrees to. Accordingly, terms proliferate, but their meanings remain distinct. An ordinary dictionary will yield fairly clear definitions of such words as absurd, burlesque, caricature, comedy, comic, farce, grotesque, humor, irony, nonsense, parody, repartee, sarcasm, sardonic, satire, travesty, and wit. Sometimes, as in the case of "wit" or "comic," the meaning becomes more complex, but it is bounded, and you can trace it with the aid of, say, Fowler's *Modern English Usage* or some of the writers on the comic who have taken on the worthy task of clarifying terms.[3]

Despite the incompleteness of Aristotle's remarks on comedy, sixteenth-century Italian humanists, caught up in the early Renaissance enthusiasm for all things newly rediscovered from the Greek, elaborated and developed lots of Aristotelian theories of comedy,[4] and these theories lasted well into the eighteenth century. Later theorists then multiplied explanations of laughter to the point where the mere bibliographies of theories require a bibliography of their own.[5] Others go beyond bibliography and anthologize joke types or theories. Still others are tempted, as I am, by an elusive will-o'-the-wisp, some glimmering of commonality in all these theories, to try to organize them into a coherent whole or to sort them into meaningful divisions.[6]

Others, confronted with this theoretical Tower of Babel, simply give up the possibility of theory or definition.[7] As the philosopher of fluidity, Benedetto Croce, said, "Who will ever logically determine the dividing line between the comic and the
non-comic, between laughter and smiles, between smiling and
gravity, or cut the ever varying continuum into which life melts
into closely divided parts?" Or we might thump the table with
the redoubtable Dr. Johnson: "Any man's reflections will inform him, that every dramatic composition which raises mirth
is comick."

I prefer to puzzle further, and I would start to sort out the
atticful of theories I have collected by observing that laughing
seems to me the perfect subject for showing that our relation to
literature, indeed to life itself, is dialectic. By that word, I want
to imply only that when we respond to the world, stimulus
and response do not have any simple cause-and-effect relationship. Rather stimulus "causes" response only as one side in a
dialogue prompts another: it cues a response without deter-
mining its particular form. Laughter takes us by surprise, yes,
but it is the same sort of surprise that we feel at our own
sudden imaginings. Our amusement defines a joke as a joke as
much as the joke defines our amusement.

Philosophers less firmly committed to the "common-sense
view" than, say, Dr. Johnson make some such dialectic relationship between ourselves and reality the heart of their philoso-
phies. They are apt therefore to give rather elaborate disquisi-
tions on why we laugh. Similarly, the dialectic between self
and other or self and society stands at the core of the psychologist's, the anthropologist's, and the psychoanalyst's enterprise.
They, too, develop theories of laughter. Others, less subtle,
pass by the temptations of dialectic and consider only one side
of laughter: the joke, the timing, the bodily act of laughing.
Even these simpler theorists, though, have to find a way to
balance comic stimulus against the response of laughter.

Thus the seemingly simple question "Why do we laugh?"
really leads into much more complicated questions about how

we perceive, how we decide what is real, and how we share values, methods, ideas—and jokes—with others. To ask, "Why do we laugh?" is also to ask, "How can we ask, 'Why do we laugh?'" And that is why the first part of this book, surveying theories, leads to a second part. Once the theories are brought together, I can ask what frame I can put around them within which they can explain better than they have. In particular, how can we confront the individuality of our amusement? How can we reconcile that individuality with theories that try to categorize jokes and laughings? What does the reason I laugh have to do with the reason "we" laugh—if there is any such thing?

But first the theories. We can parcel the comic into five segments. The comic stimulus—what do we find funny? Comic conditions—under what circumstances *don't* we find something funny? The psychology of the comic—what goes on in our minds when we feel something is funny? The physiology of the comic—what goes on in our bodies? The comic catharsis—what is the effect after we have been amused? To each a chapter.

2 *Stimuli*

The question is: What do we find funny? What attributes of a thing do we think of as comic? In other words, we are looking to the laugh*able* and not the laugh*er* for why we laugh.

Just about anybody who develops a theory of the laughable begins with the idea of *incongruity*. Many simply stop with that large idea. Others specify.

They say, for example, that people laugh at an incongruity between the way they see the object now and the way they know it from some earlier time. People laugh at a "descending" incongruity between "great things and small"—that was Herbert Spencer's theory. People laugh at a big incongruity, at disproportion, "as a man with an immoderate long nose, or a very short one (no nose at all would raise our horror)"—that was a theory of Joseph Priestley, who used his nose to discover oxygen. People laugh when they discover an unexpected likeness between things that otherwise seem unlike—that was a popular theory during the eighteenth century, a general definition of "wit."[1]

As I sort out these theorists of the laughable, they speak of three general kinds of incongruity. You could call them cognitive, ethical, and formal.

Cognitive Incongruity

Cognitive incongruities speak to our intellects. Theorists who believe that people laugh when they sense a cognitive incongruity say such things as: You laugh when something affirms and denies the same proposition simultaneously. You laugh when something creates disorder and then quickly and happily resolves that disorder. You laugh at the contrast between a gratifying organization and an annoying disorganization. You laugh at the incongruity between an intellectual contradiction and an emotional reaction to it. You laugh if something presents the limitations of our real world as a way to affirm the logical order of some other, ideal plane.[2] All such incongruities work with our acts of knowing.

The incongruity might be the jarring of two or more values. We laugh, perhaps, when something is valued and disvalued at the same time, for example, when a person is treated as a thing, as in a slapstick routine at the circus. In such a maneuver, the comic can come close to horror—the Holocaust treated people as things—and we do often laugh in horror movies.[3] Even so, I do not see how the Holocaust can be comical, no matter how laughable Frankenstein and Dracula are. (But then there was Mel Brooks's side-splitting movie *The Producers*, with its cheery song "Springtime for Hitler.")

Cognitive incongruities may touch on social issues. We can laugh at two conflicting values in the social order which apply equally to the same social situation. This theory covers that classic comic character, the Fool. He loosens all the human and social boundaries. He is both boasting man and simpering woman, willful and helpless, wise and foolish, disciplined and chaotic, shaped and shapeless.[4]

Ethical Incongruity

Ethical incongruities appeal more explicitly to our sense of values. This theory says we laugh when we see the incongruity between the noble and the contemptible, the high and the low, the sacred and the profane, the splendid and the scorned— finally, good and evil. The theory comes ultimately, I think, from Plato. He held that the comic lies in the acting out of the

opposite of the Delphic oracle's injunction: "Know *not* thyself."
As Ralph Waldo Emerson put it, we laugh at the contrast between "the ideal of right and truth" and "the yawning delin-
quencies of practice." We laugh at the contrast between someone's invented self, which is aspiring, glorified, or affected,
and the factual self of body and appetite.[5]

According to these theories the funny can simply be the objective reporting of such a discrepancy, and so it was for such
great neoclassic comic writers as Jonathan Swift and Henry
Fielding. Fielding took as his butt "affectation," which he intended in a very broad, Platonic sense as any instance of seem-
ing to be one thing when one is actually something else. In this
vein, humor can become a reaction against hypocrisy. All he
had to do was represent a person with a foible displaying that
foible as intensely as possible. Or you could define humor as
the chronicling of people's failures to live up to standards of
excellence, either their own or those set by society.[6]

The laughable, seen as an ethical congruity, can seem very
static, even fixed. Accordingly, in 1900, writing under the influence of the theory of evolution, Henri Bergson proposed
one of the most famous and successful explanations of laughter. I think of it as a modification of Plato's theory: Bergson
replaced the perhaps static Platonic ideal (contrasted to the
less than ideal) with the rush of life, the *élan vital*. For Bergson, the comic became "a certain mechanical inelasticity just
where one would expect to find the wide-awake adaptability
and the living pliableness of a human being." The comic finds
such contradictions when people specialize too much or when
our conventions do not allow for something.[7] Bergson's idea
works perfectly for the comedy of his contemporary George
Bernard Shaw, who always contrasted the sterile, hidebound,
conventional, pedantic, or capitalist with the living, loving re-
production of human beings fulfilling their destiny in biological
evolution.

Other theorists have generalized ethical incongruity in other
directions: the contrast between a perception and an image or

between a means and an end, between the high and the low, the noteworthy and the commonplace, between solemn speech and street slang.[8]

Still others have suggested a contrast between beauty and the laughable. According to the idealist philosophers of the nineteenth century, beauty comes from the unity of an idea (loosely, an ideal) and its physical opposite. We feel the sublime, they said, when the idea triumphs over the physical, but we laugh when the physical becomes detached from the idea.[9] Perhaps the German philosopher Schopenhauer was echoing this belief when he defined the laughable as the incongruity between a concept and the real object to which it was designed to relate. Thus Schopenhauer found irresistibly funny the question "What is the angle between a circle and its tangent?" He was indeed a German philosopher.

Most other writers who have drawn on the Platonic theory of the laughable as ethical incongruity have tended to limit the laughable to the specifically human. Circles and angles could be funny only to the extent that they resemble human beings.

Formal Incongruity

Under "formal incongruity" I put the theories of the funny that stem from Aristotle. Comedy, said Aristotle, "consists in some defect," and he used the same word as for the "tragic flaw" that gives rise to tragedy, *hamartia*, "some defect or ugliness which is not painful or destructive." We could put it more succinctly: something harmful presented harmlessly. Essentially, then, Aristotle, in dividing literature into the comic and the epic-tragic, divides it into the playful, where imperfections do not hurt, and the serious, where they do. He translated this distinction into dramatic terms by insisting that comedy must deal with "meaner" (perhaps he meant typical) humans, while tragedy must deal with "noble" (unusual?) people. In tragedy, we look up to the characters. In comedy, we look down on them.

Aristotle's theory that we laugh at the contrast between the thing presented and the way it is presented marks a notable sophistication (I think) over cognitive and ethical theories, which limit themselves to the subject matter of the laughable. Aristotle opens up the question of literary form.

Perhaps that is why Aristotle's theory has proved so impressively durable. Julius Caesar echoed it (as reported by Cicero). So did Molière, when he said that comedies "render agreeably on a stage the faults of all mankind." Neoclassic writers suggested that the comic consisted of linking the admirable to the base or the beautiful to the deformed or the plausible to the absurd.[10] Aristotle's idea also lends itself to theories of play: the comic combines the discipline of art with the lack of discipline in play.[11]

In Romantic and post-Romantic times, theorists of the comic have pointed Aristotle's theory of formal incongruity back toward the thing presented. The laughable presents something like a defect or failure, but harmlessly. For example, one German theorist wrote of "that little thing which behaves as though it were a big one, that swells itself to do it, that plays the role of a big thing and then behaves again like a little thing or melts into something insignificant."[12] (I find his hint that the phallus is the prototype of the laughable itself laughable.)

Luigi Pirandello gives Aristotle's theory a postmodern turn. He speaks of a feeling of contrariness that follows one's more normal emotions as a shadow follows the body. "Ordinarily, the artist concerns himself only with the body. The humorist," and I think Pirandello must have meant the kind of metadramatist _he_ was, "the humorist concerns himself with body and shadow at the same time and sometimes more with the shadow than the body. He notes all the fine turns of that shadow, how it stretches this much or grows that much fatter, as if to make fun of the body, which all this time does not concern itself with the shadow or its size."

Our age also turns Aristotle's idea into a psychological one. Max Eastman's book on laughter, written in reaction to the early influence of Sigmund Freud, created a stir in the 1920s. He suggested that jokes combined playful disappointment with satisfaction. They built on people's ability "to make the best of a bad thing . . . an act of aggressive resignation." The poet W. H. Auden spoke (less wittily than usual) of a "contradiction in the relation of the individual or the personal to the universal or the impersonal which does not involve the spectator or hearer in suffering or pity" (and I suppose that "pity" provides the clue to Aristotle's presence).[13]

Inevitably, within this psychologizing, behaviorist theories arise, treating joking and other "verbal behavior" as embodying the jokemaker's responses to stimuli which then become stimuli to our response—laughter. Says B. F. Skinner, we find verbal behavior funny if it combines a strong and a weak response. We will laugh if one stimulus-response embodied in the joke is strong or regular, the kind of thing to which one would say, "I understand" or "That makes sense," and the other element is weak or far-fetched, something from the fringes of the verbal field. He notes, "Polysyllabic rhymes are likely to be far-fetched in this sense." Although Skinner uses the language of "response" here, it seems to me he is writing something very like an Aristotelian description of the stimulus: something strong weakly presented.

The theories from gestalt psychology also seem to me crypto-Aristotelian. In a gestalt framework, humor is produced by a change in the configuration in which an element plays a part. Thus, according to Gregory Bateson, when we appreciate a joke, we are doing something like responding to a shift in the relationship between figure and ground. An element that had seemed to be part of the background is now seen as "figure," as newly crucial. Laughter oscillates in a ha-ha-ha, because it comes from paradoxes or figure-ground shifts that have a "circuit" quality. Within a Batesonian framework, humor uses many other paradoxes to mesh with and reinforce the fundamental paradox: humor sets up a "play frame." Within it, we know that a given action does not stand for the behavior it usually represents. It is "only" a joke. What had seemed central—figure—becomes ground.[14]

A semiotic analysis of laughter would be even more fashionably modern than Bateson's gestalt theory, but only one theorist has taken this tack. G. B. Milner begins by introducing the idea of a universe of discourse from logic and linguistics. (A "topic," one might say.) He suggests that the stimulus to laughter consists of the collision of two normally quite distinct universes of discourse within a single context. Generally, he says, some trick of language or situation, some reversal or transposition, makes the two topics collide, and we laugh. A pun, for example, reverses the usual and expected word so as to make like ideas unlike or unlike ideas like. Similarly, a spoonerism inverts the usual, expected structure to the same effect. "Time wounds all heels."

Milner calls a reversal of the word "paradigmatic" and a reversal of structure "syntagmatic." Most jokes, he says, confuse these paradigmatic and syntagmatic axes. They mix up, say, the metaphorical and the actual, as in Groucho Marx's "When I came to this country I hadn't a nickel in my pocket. Now I have a nickel in my pocket." Behind all these reversals, says Milner, stands the human tension beween nature and culture, deeply rooted in the unconscious. We are laughing because we suddenly see a new set of differential relations. Hidden patterns rise to the surface. (One of those hidden patterns, surely, includes the dressing up of an ancient incongruity theory in newfangled jargon.)

The novelist and polymath Arthur Koestler offers a useful metaphor for the incongruous juxtaposition of ideas. He describes the process as following down one train of thought while another is visible in the background. Suddenly you come to a junction where the two tracks intersect. The figure of speech enables Koestler to show that you can reverse incongruities or jokes. A miser who heard the water running in his house rushed downstairs and into the street shouting, "I'm being robbed! Someone is taking a bath." The first train of thought is property and its theft: "miser," "robbed." The second train is taking a bath, and the junction is the word "taking." We can reverse the two trains of thought, following down baths. One thief was standing next to another and he noticed a peculiar odor. "Say," he said, "have you taken a bath lately?" "Why?" said the other. "Is one missing?" The reversal works better, Koestler notes, if the two lines of thought bear some closer relation to one another than baths and property. (And any joke works better if it's not in a book that is asking you why you laugh.)

Koestler's train metaphor and the semiotic theory take us back from the specialized cognitive, ethical, and formal incongruities to the first and simplest idea. We laugh when we see an incongruity. One could multiply almost indefinitely the list of theorists, from ancient times to the most modern, who state this stimulus-response theory of laughter. As it becomes more and more difficult to be original, writers simply elaborate some category that will include all the different variants of "incongruity" or some one incongruity to which you can reduce all the others. To be sure, when I read over and over again about sudden contrasts between the particular and the general, between organization and disorganization, aspiration and fact, high and low, big and small, I do get a feeling there must be some one incongruity that will include all the others.

On the other hand, we laugh in so many different circumstances that it seems doubtful we can reduce all laughter to a single cause. Also, these theories are truly "reductive." They convert all the richness of a *Don Quixote* or a *Decameron* to the same thing—incongruity—happening over and over again. They leave out the careful analysis of the funny work itself and settle for filing it in a theoretical pigeonhole: incongruity of one kind or another.[15]

Also, they leave out the differences in our response. Why *didn't* you find the joke about the thieves and the bath funny? (It appears in all the standard books.) Had you read it before?

Was it too slow? All these incongruity theories assume that the joke (or any literary work, really) acts as a stimulus to produce a standardized response. The semioticist Milner even says, "We do not laugh, but 'something laughs in us.'" What happens, then, to "'Tain't funny, McGee"?

Yet this impersonal conclusion was inevitable. Given a stimulus-response model of humor, we must all be alike as pigeons on the grass—alas. There is, however, one obvious way of taking individual differences into account, such as your having heard the one about the thieves and the bath before. We can consider differences in the conditions under which we meet these various incongruities.

3 Conditions

To say that a comic stimulus such as incongruity in and of itself "causes" a comic result (be it a smile, laughter, or simply an amused feeling), we have to believe there are guaranteed sure-fire humdingers that will never fail to get a laugh even from a mugger's victim lying bloodied in the street. That seems an unpromising hypothesis.

We can, however, shore up the incongruity theories by qualifying them. Comic stimuli do "cause" comic responses—if the conditions are right. Usually people talk about these conditions only in connection with laughter, but I think they can be applied with equal propriety to the comic in general. That is, a thing isn't funny unless it makes us feel like laughing, even if we don't actually guffaw. Within this set of assumptions, the two most commonly stated conditions are play and timing.

Play

We feel the comic only in playful situations, not in those we take seriously.[1] Why is a situation playful, then? As you might expect, theorists have provided lots of answers.

A situation may be playful because we need not fear for ourselves—as novelist John Updike concludes: "Laughter, then, can be construed as a signal of danger past or dismissed . . . within an arena, whether the arms of a mother or the covers of a novel, where the customary threats of life have been suspended."

Alternatively, we may feel playful because we do not fear for another. "The comic," says Bergson, in his famous phrasing, "demands something like a momentary anaesthesia of the heart." Or as comedian Mel Brooks puts the matter, passing a harsh judgment on humankind: "Tragedy is if I cut my finger. Comedy is if you walk into an open sewer and die."[2]

One can take "play" in the narrow sense of "playful." You can also make it a very broad concept, as the great theorist of play, Johann Huizinga, has done:

> a free activity standing quite consciously outside 'ordinary' life as being 'not serious,' but at the same time absorbing the player intensely and utterly. It is an activity connected with no material interest, and no profit can be gained by it. It proceeds within its own proper boundaries of time and space according to fixed rules and in an orderly manner. It promotes the formation of social groupings which tend to surround themselves with secrecy and to stress their difference from the common world.

Play, in this large, sociological sense, includes games, rituals, drama, and perhaps all the formalities that touch on love, law, war, or poetry.

One can also define the formality of play psychologically, for example, by these two criteria: objectivity—one's emotions and sympathies are unengaged and isolation—the logic of the play, game, or joke applies only to that situation and therefore need not be applied realistically. More simply stated, the conditions for the comic are compactness, mechanism, and exaggeration.[3] Think of tournaments or chess or courtly love. If rules and distancing define play, then I can understand Bergson's claim that "our laughter is always the laughter of a group." "It must have a *social* signification."

Arthur Koestler suggests that there must be "economy" in the text and an "implicit riddle character."[4] The problem is, as we say, to "get" the joke. Here, with riddles, we touch on play and ritual. To primitive societies, riddles are important ways of knowing things. Indeed, the word comes from a Teutonic root meaning "counsel." (Poor Aethelred the Unready was just badly advised—*anræde.*) Primitive societies—like literary critics today—engage in elaborate puzzle contests and witty controversies and debates. Certain mythological heroes, such as Oedipus and Theseus, have as their major claim to that exalted status some outstanding feat of riddle solving.

Timing

As early as the sixteenth century people began to point to suddenness, unexpectedness, and (particularly) surprise as indispensable prerequisites to laughter. Sustained humor, then, such as *Don Quixote* or the *Decameron*, would reduce simply to a series of comic surprises.[5]

Making surprise a precondition of laughter explains why jokes get old and why they don't amuse the teller. In either case, the "punch" is telegraphed, and we lack the essential surprise.

It is even possible to argue that the condition is more important than the stimulus, that timing is the one thing that differentiates the tragic from the comic. A tragedy is just a comedy slowed down, you could say. Conversely, if we speed tragic or "serious" things up, they get funny (as Mack Sennett recognized). We can laugh at the most serious music in the world if the record is played at 78 rpm instead of 33 1/3, and, conversely, a pratfall in slow motion ceases to be funny. If a silent movie of *Hamlet* were projected at sound speed, we would get a kind of Keystone Kop comedy (the bumbling pursuit of a criminal). Many tragedies have joke situations at their core: the man who blinded himself because he heard that blind people had more insight (Oedipus), the prince who couldn't pull himself together, so he kept taking other people apart (Hamlet),[6] or the man who "pared [his] wit o' both sides, and left nothing in the middle" (King Lear). Notice how in translating a tragedy into a

joke one makes the personages "low," or at least universal, as
Aristotle insisted they be for comedy.

Assigning preconditions such as playfulness and timing to
the laughable helps open the fairly rigid idea of a comic stimulus to the variability of people's laughter and failure to laugh.
I think we need something more, however. How can we account for the variability of audience response under identical
conditions of timing and playfulness? In a theater, for example,
dozens of people may be bored even though hundreds are
amused. We need, I think, a psychology of the comic, and
theorists have not been slow to provide it—lots of them.

4 *Psychology*

Over the centuries, a great many psychologists have had a go at laughter. I can distinguish four large groups of psychological theories about the comic, based on archetypes, conscious feelings, psychoanalysis, and experiments. They vary widely in the complexity of the answers they give and in the kinds of human laws they presuppose. Unlike the theories based on stimulus and conditions, all psychological theories locate the source of the laughable in some sort of transaction between the laugher and the laughed-at instead of in the laughed-at alone. And all assume considerable uniformity among people. Otherwise, I suppose, they might not be psychologies.

Archetype Theories

Some of the most interesting thinkers about the comic in the last seventy years or so have worked under the influence of Freud, Carl Jung, and those classicists who, following Gilbert Murray, have chosen to look at Greece anthropologically. The facts about Greek rituals come from folk customs, from archaeological discoveries, from whatever sources can be found that will shed light on the unrecorded activities of primitive peoples. Frequently, of course, the evidence reveals as much about the modern researcher's enthusiasms as those of prehistoric humans.

The basic psychological hypothesis in this study of ritual is that early humans used rituals to act out aspects of their being for their own satisfaction and understanding. Though such rituals may become atrophied, disguised, or vestigial, they persist because they express the enduring, archetypal mysteries of birth, death, and sexuality, of seedtime and harvest, of the cycles of day and night and the seasons. Many aspects of modern life, including comedy and the comic, build on these rituals and, so the theory says, continue their age-old appeal. That is, a comic work that draws on these ancient rituals taps universal archetypes in us, causing us to resonate with some deep source of hidden vitality.

I sort comic rituals into three basic archetypes. The first seems to turn up everywhere: death and rebirth, the fertility ritual, the lesson of the seed. Its pattern is: challenge; struggle and defeat; final victory. It imitates all those rhythms in our lives which end, after an apparent blackout, in some final recovery and resolution: war and peace, winter and spring, sleep and waking, death and life after death, the sexual act—in short, all those things that prove that something must "die" so that something new may come into being.

The prototype of the death-and-rebirth ritual is the sacrifice: a totem animal, a *pharmakos*, or a scapegoat (human or animal) is magically loaded with the sins of the community, then sacrificed by the community and mourned. The sacrifice rises to the gods and the community is "reborn," that is, cleansed.[1]

The basic death-and-rebirth plot builds on a conflict (*agon*) between a protagonist (spring, life, the New Year, the new king, the new god, the man of light, the son, the tribesman) who seems to be less than he is and an antagonist (winter, death, old year, old king, old god, man of darkness, the father, the totem animal) who pretends to be more than he is and who tries to block the progress represented by the protagonist. In the first round of their fight, the antagonist wins. The protagonist is killed and may be eaten. Then the protagonist is reborn, drives off the antagonist, is worshiped as a god—and may be married.[2]

The pattern, of course, has many variations. One common one makes the ritual into an initiation in which a child or naif is taken away from the group, often by means of a long walk, and after some ordeal is symbolically "killed" (marked, wounded, circumcised, or put to sleep). Then he is shown sacred objects, questioned about them, and returned to the tribe as an adult member. In the fertility ritual itself, banishment can substitute for killing: werewolf myths come from the banishing of a man disguised as the totem animal, whom it is death to look upon. In another variation, the *agon* may be made a purely verbal battle of invective. Thus Aristotle reports that the first comic writers wrote simple invectives. These verbal contests, logomachies, eventually ceased to be ritual and became secular satire, purely literary.[3]

Tragedy (in its strict sense) is only the first half of the death-and-rebirth pattern, as Northrop Frye has pointed out. "Tragedy is really implicit or uncompleted comedy; . . . comedy contains a potential tragedy within itself."[4] In one frequent tragic variation, protagonist and antagonist are compressed into one man with a better half and a tragic "flaw," frequently pride—the antagonist's pretense that he is more than he is.

To give comedy its due weight in this comparison, one should remember that the two great ages of Western tragedy did not allow a tragedy to end with catastrophe. Greek tragedy took the form of a trilogy (reflecting the three stages of the ritual drama) which proceeded to "an essentially comic resolution," in which the hero's sin was expiated. The trilogy itself was followed by a funny, and very lewd, satyr play.[5] Similarly, Elizabethan tragedies never ended simply with the death of the protagonist, because society must always be brought back to normality. Elizabethan tragedies contained comic counterparts to the "serious" plot and were almost always followed on stage by a comic jig. Tragedy, then, branched off from the basic ritual plot by emphasizing the struggle and death. Comedy emphasized the rebirth and marriage.

In the West, our oldest surviving comedy is the Old Comedy of Aristophanes. These plays (and Aristotle's meager comments on them) still show the ritual structure fairly clearly, as do the tragedies of the period (fifth and early fourth centuries). The New Comedy of Menander (late fourth century) seems to be, says Northrop Frye, "a realistic foreshortening of a death-and-resurrection pattern, in which the struggle and rebirth of a divine hero has shrunk into a marriage, the freeing of a slave, and the triumph of a young man over an older one."[6] Plautus and Terence copied Menander to make Roman comedy. From them New Comedy passed into the unwritten Italian *commedia dell'arte*, which influenced Shakespeare, Ben Jonson, Molière, and indeed all later comedy.

During Christian times, the concept of the *felix culpa* (the happy fault) developed from pagan ritual. People decided they could look on Adam's fall (as on the tragic hero's defeat) as a blessing in disguise, for it led to God's priceless gift of rebirth through Christ. Pagan ritual elements became fused in Christian rituals, and thence in Christian tragedy and comedy, becoming finally the great concept of the *commedia*, the Divine Comedy of sin and redemption.[7]

Any and all of these shadings, pagan and Christian, may be found in post-Renaissance comedy. Virtually all comedy, however, retains the old fertility drama in its basic comic plot structure: situation, complication, and resolution.

The characters as well as the plot structure of the ritual fertility drama lasted into later comedy. The protagonist, the "white man," Xanthos, was an *eiron*, that is, an ironical man who seemed to be less than he was. A companion, the buffoon, helped him and played tricks on everybody; he also pretended to be less than he was. From these two come all the later fools, jesters, Pierrots, and clowns (painted the white of death), who pretend to be the least of men, but who are actually wiser than most and sometimes are credited with supernatural powers of prophecy. They seem free, but the audience knows they are limited and must die. Even so, they seem to survive every beating and adversity they suffer as scapegoats. Aristotle used Socrates as an example of the *eiron* (an evaluation corresponding to Aristotle's general opinion that Plato did not give proper value to concrete reality). More immediately, the buffoon became the witty slave of New Comedy and the witty servant in Shakespeare, Jonson, and Molière.[8]

The antagonist, the blocking character, the "black man," Melanthos, was an *alazon*, a man who pretended to be more than he was (his blackness symbolizing not only death, but also disguise, frequently disguise as the totem animal). He was accompanied by the "impostor," an alter ego. Thus later comedy almost always attacks pretensions, "affectation" in Fielding's sense: the dissembling Vices of medieval comedy, the preposterously boastful Falstaff and Wife of Bath and the *augusto* of the European circus (as in Ingmar Bergman's *Clown's Evening* and Federico Fellini's *Clowns*).

From these two ancient types later drama developed a full cast. From the *eiron* and buffoon came the "young man" (the hero, handsome, virile, the one we can identify with, the one who gets the girl at the end), the "parasite" (his servant, who steals wit, glory, money, sex, and, in general, anything within reach), and a pedant or doctor (a figure lean, pale, not of this world, who originally helped to bring the ritual hero back to life). From the *alazon* and impostor come the "old man" (the *senex*, testy, impotent, rustic, stingy, and restrictive), the "old woman" (the *kordax*, ugly, drunk, and amorous), and the swaggering soldier (or *miles gloriosus*, a braggart who is shown up). Two other characters have ambiguous origins: the cook (connected with the ritual eating of the hero) and a silent young woman (married to the *eiron* at the end).[9]

A modern version of the *eiron-alazon* struggle is "The Honeymooners," the television skits with the bluff, boasting Jackie

Gleason and the dry, fey, seemingly foolish Art Carney. An ancient one is the Socratic dialogue. For Plato, the incongruity between what is and what ought to be represented not just the comic, but the most basic assumption of his philosophy. He dramatized this discrepancy by playing off the idealized *eiron* Socrates, the riddle solver, the man who looks beyond this world, against the very real and very inadequate persons of the dialogues, who tend to overstate themselves, who think they know all the answers. Indeed, the Greeks themselves seem to have considered the Platonic dialogues to be *comic* works.[10] So understood, Socrates' death takes on a new shading. As the philosophical hero of the new age of abstract symbols and concepts, Socrates reenacts the scapegoat-hero of the age of myth. He suffers a ritual killing and apotheosis at the hands of his community in the archetypal comic plot of death and rebirth. It is significant in this context that Socrates placed foremost among his accusers "a comic poet," a reference to Aristophanes' burlesque of Socrates in *The Clouds*.

The most common comic pattern seems to be death and resurrection. I think the second most common is the feast. It imitates our all too human chafing at social rules and symbolizes our longing to return to a golden age when there was no need for them. A feast propitiates our cruder impulses.

These feasts may be related to the fertility ritual either as the symbolic eating of the sacrificed hero or as the marriage feast at the end. Such feasts are institutionalized all over the world— the Greek Dionysia, the Roman Saturnalia, the medieval Feast of Fools, Renaissance Maypole games, the carnivals (*carne vale*, O flesh! farewell) before Lent, the Tibetan King of the Years' ten days of misrule, and our own New Year's Eve, rather feeble by comparison. Such rites penetrated even monasteries. In medieval times Friar Juniper, the holy clown of the Franciscan order, would preside over a *festus fatuorum*, a feast of fools, where

priests and clerks may be seen wearing masks and monstrous
visages at the hours of office. They dance in the choir dressed as
women, panders, or minstrels. They sing wanton songs. They
eat black puddings at the horn of the altar while the celebrant is
saying mass. They play at dice there. They cense with stinking
smoke from the soles of old shoes. They run and leap through
the church without a blush at their own shame. Finally they
drive about the town and its theatre in shabby traps and carts;
and rouse the laughter of their fellows and the by-standers in
infamous performances, with indecent gestures and verses scur-
rilous and unchaste.[11]

These feasts could be (in less uneasily religious ages than our
own) quite licentious and orgiastic. They almost always contained an element of parody of existing institutions of government or religion. Nothing was too sacred to be turned upside
down and mocked. Customarily, the community elected a Lord
of Misrule to preside over the merriment. This individual, too,
stemmed from the fool or clown, the *eiron* of the archetypal
drama. He was granted great privileges, treated as a king or
pontiff (remember that the fool carried a scepter and wore a
kind of crown), but might be symbolically "killed" as part of
the festivities.[12]

In comic literature, the feast becomes comic license. We allow poets to set up a comic world in which everything is topsy-
turvy and none of the rules of everyday life apply, only joke
rules; a world where all the bludgeons are rubber and the most
horrible punishment is to be laughed at. Shakespeare's comic
purgations take place in green worlds of "mad mistaking": the
forest of Arden, the "wood near Athens," Illyria, Bohemia,
Prospero's island, where everything is all mixed up but everything comes out all right, and everybody is better for it.[13] So,
too, Molière's characters, even in the heart of Paris, bear the
names of conventional shepherds and shepherdesses.

The comic uses still a third ritual possibility, marriage. It
imitates the linking of high to low, sun to soil, rain to earth,
male to female, God to humanity, the king to his people:

I will greatly rejoice in the Lord, my soul shall be joyful in my God; for he hath clothed me with the garments of salvation, he hath covered me with the robe of righteousness, as a bridegroom decketh himself with ornaments, and as a bride adorneth herself with her jewels. For as the earth bringeth forth her bud, and as the garden causeth the things that are sown in it to spring forth; so the Lord God will cause righteousness and praise to spring forth before all the nations.[14]

Such phrasings may recall Stone Age times, when, some feminists believe, with the discovery of seeds and regular planting, woman became custodian of the means of food production. Rituals came into being to celebrate the marriage of the sun god to the moon mother goddess. The rite frequently took place in a cattle byre or hut, and the cow mother was identified with the seed-bearing tree.[15] Woman, so understood, can appear in any of three forms: the virgin Artemis, the fruitful mother Aphrodite, or Atropos, the crone who is the custodian of the dead.

Cults of the mother goddess spread far and wide in the Near East during the Graeco-Roman period, as described, for example, by Apuleius in his novel *The Golden Ass*, which he built on the rituals of Isis worship. Some phrases from Isis worship even became embedded in the Roman Missal, the antiphons for the feast of the Assumption of the Blessed Virgin Mary (August 15). Marriage became an ending for the fertility ritual: a mute woman (the earth goddess) appeared and was married to the *eiron*.[16]

Myth-and-ritual readings of modern comic literature trace the way patterns from prehistoric times apparently persist, often in such striking particulars as marriage to a silent woman in Ben Jonson's comedy of that name, the Western hero's white hat, and the march of green, fertile Birnam Wood against sterile, killing Macbeth. The usual explanation is that we inherit—in broad outline, anyway—archetypes of myth and ritual. Therefore literary experiences fall naturally into those patterns. Given the way that many birds inherit knowledge of their species' twittering, given that many mammals inherit as much or more, I think it possible that we inherit ideas about black, white, vegetation, and irony.

It makes more sense to me, however, to think that we sustain or recreate these narrative patterns within the larger biological patterns all or many humans share. Each of us absorbs these story forms through birth, being mothered, growing, adolescence, love, work, sex, fathering or mothering (sometimes), aging and dying (certainly). "Comedy is an art form that arises naturally wherever people are gathered to celebrate life, in spring festivals, triumphs, birthdays, weddings, or initiations. It is an image of human vitality holding its own in the world amid the surprises of unplanned coincidence . . . [and] thanks or challenges to fortune," writes Susanne Langer.[17]

But where do the details come from? One can trace a direct line of imitation from a dramatist such as Shaw to Molière to *commedia dell'arte* to Roman comedy and so back to the fertility rituals that underlay the Old Comedy. *Hello, Dolly!* runs back through Thornton Wilder's *Matchmaker* and *Merchant of Yonkers*, which are conscious imitations of Roman comedy. Marcel Carné's *Enfants du Paradis* uses *commedia dell'arte* explicitly. Hence I am not surprised that it makes its heroine into a mother goddess. Can one account for *all* ancient echoes in modern comedies this way? And their details? The three generations of women in Ingmar Bergman's *Smiles of a Summer Night* and in Robert Altman's *3 Women*? The bacchanalia in Federico Fellini's *Dolce Vita*? It seems, indeed, faintly possible. But why do the moderns imitate the ancient patterns? And why do audiences seem to like it when they do? There is as much mystery here as solution to mystery.

Psychologies of Consciousness

In contrast to theories based on deep archetypes in a collective unconscious stand the common-sense psychologies, those that systematize our conscious experience. Applied to laughter and the comic, they yield two characteristic explanations: relief and superiority.

For a long time, people have noticed that the comic is a relaxation or release of pent-up energy. Max Beerbohm remarked, as a practicing wit, "To have good reason for not laughing is one of the surest aids." "Laughter rejoices in bonds." And every teacher somewhat blushingly knows how easy it is to get a laugh from bored, restless—and restrained—students.

Immanuel Kant's theory operates at a more intellectual level: "Laughter is an affectation arising from a sudden transformation of a strained expectation into nothing." The experience is one of relief: at a false alarm, at deceived expectation, at finding one need not expend a large effort of comprehension, or perhaps "a reversal of what was right up till then the customary and expected." The body, having prepared for action on the world, expends itself instead in action by or in the body itself. Or perhaps laughter is a social signal to other members of the group that they can relax with safety.[18]

Thus laughter occurs when the same situation induces both alarm and a quite contradictory attitude of playfulness or indifference. Prototypes are the jack-in-the-box, the roller coaster, and tickling.[19] William Hazlitt spells the idea out:

> The serious is the habitual stress which the mind lays upon the expectation of a given order of events, following one another with a certain regularity and weight of interest attached to them. When this stress is increased . . . it becomes the pathetic or tragical. The ludicrous, or comic, is the unexpected loosening or relaxing this stress below its usual pitch of intensity by such an abrupt transposition of the order of our ideas, as taking the mind unawares, throws it off its guard, startles it into a lively sense of pleasure, and leaves no time nor inclination for painful reflections.

Kant and Hazlitt represent one kind of relief theory. In another, one might accent not the emotional relief, but the cognitive solution. Thus John Dewey held that laughter is the pleasure of suddenly attaining unity at the end of a period of suspense, or, as a French theorist put it, "putting objects in categories that suit them better than our customary categories." The psychologist D. E. Berlyne sees "arousal" as the key, coming from "collative" factors, that is, attempts to collate experience despite novelty, surprise, incongruity, strangeness, complexity, ambiguity, puzzlement, or contradiction. Then we get "some factor that signifies safety, readjustment, clarification, or release."[20]

Relief theories of this kind seem to me simply to psychologize incongruity theories of the stimulus. Or vice versa. Thus the eighteenth-century scientist Joseph Priestley derived incongruity in the object from relief in the subject. "Laughter when it first appears in children . . . is a *nascent cry*, raised by pain, or the apprehension of pain, suddenly checked, and repeated at very short intervals." The checked cry becomes habit until "almost any brisk emotion or surprise suddenly checked, and recurring alternately, will produce it; and at last any strong opposition, or contrast in things. . . ."[21]

In 1650, however, philosopher Thomas Hobbes went beyond relief to produce one of the most famous formulas of the comic. In a way, you could think of him as refining the idea of relief by describing the nature of the tension and the nature of the release: "The passion of laughter is nothing else but sudden glory arising from sudden conception of some eminency in ourselves, by comparison with the infirmity of others, or with our own formerly." Beware the man who laughs too much, Hobbes would say, for laughter "is incident most to them that are conscious of the fewest abilities in themselves; who are forced to keep themselves in their own favour by observing the imperfections of other men."[22]

Hobbes's theory helps to explain the motives and methods of the satirist; he is really laughing at his own superiority, which enables him to satirize others. (Both satire and caricature, of course, are related to magic: satire to ritual invective, and both to the disfiguring of a person's name or effigy, magically identified with the person.) Hobbes's theory also suggests a reason for the physical form laughter takes. As a theorist of the 1930s pointed out, when you have listed the significant aspects of the act of laughing (elevation of the head, baring of the teeth, emission of harsh guttural sounds), you have given the symptoms of an animal enraged.[23]

Many people have restated Hobbes's theory many times and in many ways. The inventor of *Lil Abner*, Al Capp, for example, said: "All comedy is based on man's delight in man's inhumanity to man." Joseph Addison intellectualized Hobbes: "Every one diverts himself with some Person or other that is below him in Point of Understanding, and triumphs in the Superiority of his Genius, whilst he has such Objects of Derision before his Eyes." French theorists speak of "a secret satisfaction of *amour-propre*," of "malign pleasure," and of a superiority in "manners."[24]

Identification could provide a psychological basis for Hobbes's theory: one identifies with another who shows superiority, and that other could be an idea or institution or anything that has acquired dignity. Another psychological basis could be a drive for "effectance" or mastery. The superior could establish itself as such by taking on the attributes of a general principle.[25]

Despite these extensions, Hobbes's superiority theory seems to be limited to the least savory aspects of mirth—until we realize (courtesy of Kenneth Burke) that we can state the disproportion the other way around, "calling the purpose of laughter not so much a glorifying of the self as a minimizing of the distresses menacing the self."[26]

The comic, then, is "the frustrated menace of things," according to a fervent libertarian who converts Burke's "purpose" for laughter into its cause. "I laugh at that which has endangered or degraded or has fought to suppress, enslave, or destroy what I cherish and has failed. My laughter signalizes its failure and my own liberation." Are defeated SS men funny? According to this theory, they can be, if the fear they once aroused is truly ended.[27]

Thus the comic, said an influential eighteenth-century psychologist, is "a surprise that brings on a momentary fear first, and then a momentary joy in consequence of the removal of that fear." In the twentieth century, tests have shown that tickling makes a baby laugh more if its mother does the tickling. The little one realizes more readily that the apparent threat is no threat at all. From a psychoanalytic point of view, "most comic phenomena seem to be bound up with past conflicts of the ego . . . they help it to repeat its victory and in doing so once more to overcome half-assimilated fear." Again, the one who laughs too much must have much "half-assimilated fear" to overcome.[28]

As a way of dealing with our fear or anger, laughter is adaptive. Thus Hobbes's theory admits even religious resignation: "A cartoon is funny to the degree that it reminds us that we are . . . 'mortal men,' and thereby takes the edge off our nightmares by showing that they contain an element of farce," says a former editor of *Punch*. Similarly, laughter can be an adaptive check to too much sympathy, in the sense of too great an attachment to the things and people of this world. Alternatively, laughter (still in Hobbes's general frame) is adaptive "because it calls off those impulses which arise out of anger . . . and starts back into action those impulses which belong to normal activity and normal living." Anthropologists find that joking relationships occur in a tribe when there is a basis for conflict plus principles for both conjunction and disjunction (that is, some reasons for treating certain people with respect but other reasons for treating them with familiarity). Joking achieves the right balance to keep the peace.[29]

Otherwise, Hobbes's theory is stern indeed, and there are gentler souls who would have it otherwise. Surprisingly, Voltaire was one. He recalled doubling over with laughter during his own solitary reading of Molière's *Amphitryon*. That showed, he said, that laughter does not come from "pride," for "one is not at all proud when one is alone." Oh, no?

Among those who want laughter to be gentle, Thomas Carlyle proclaims, "The essence of humour is sensibility; warm, tender fellow-feeling with all forms of existence"; "not contempt, its essence is love." "Humour," says Stephen Leacock, "may be defined as the kindly contemplation of the incongruities of life and the artistic expression thereof." Others speak of "good and pleasurable values" or a "natural unschooled goodness in the human heart."[30] At all this kindliness, I suspect, Thomas Hobbes, Charles II's "Beare," would have growled his doubts.

Psychoanalytic Theories

"Hobbes," notes one distinguished psychoanalyst, Ernst Kris, "is more akin to Freud than any later psychologist."[31] Freud's incisive monograph of 1905, *Der Witz und Seine Beziehung zum Unbewussten* (now officially translated as *Jokes and Their Relation to the Unconscious*) brings together not only Hobbes's but many other theories of the comic. In one sense, it is a synthesis. In another, however, Freud's recognition of a similarity in style between jokes and dreams (and, to a lesser extent, symptoms and slips of the tongue) meant that he could establish a relation between funniness and unconscious mental processes generally—and *that* was something new in theories of laughter, or indeed of the mind. As a result, Freud's is both more general and more precise than any previous theory of laughter.

In general, says Freud, we laugh when our minds compare two psychic processes, one complex, requiring us to spend a good deal of psychic energy to carry it out, the other simple and short-circuiting the first. The idea of comparison links Freud's psychological explanation to theories of the incongruity of the stimulus.

Freud becomes more particular than they can be, however. Within the generic term "comic" he marks out three nonexhaustive categories: jokes, the comic (used specifically, not generically), and humor. There is one easy way to distinguish them: jokes involve three persons, the comic two, and humor one.

Freud treats jokes as primarily verbal. Most of the examples he gives are puns, anecdotes, malapropisms, and the like, although a few are pictorial or physical. From an elaborate analysis of a series of examples he derives a variety of joke techniques, all of which can be put under one or more of three basic headings: (1) the use of the sound instead of the sense of a word; (2) "the rediscovery of the familiar" in a new situation; (3) the use of nonsense as a relief from the usual rules of intellectual sense. Incidentally, all of these techniques minimize threats: the tyranny of words; the fear of the new; the demands of logical thought. All of these techniques are thus comic in the Burke-Hobbes sense.

Freud notes that he has seen these techniques at work in neurotics and psychotics, in dreams, in slips of the tongue, and in the other ways in which we reveal unconscious processes. He concludes that we get a certain amount of our pleasure in jokes simply from the techniques as such. We enjoy "economy of psychic expenditure" in getting around the ordinary difficulties of thought.

Freud then distinguishes "innocent" jokes (or "jests") from "tendentious" jokes. In innocent joking, we get only the pleasure of by-passing the rules of thought. In tendentious joking, not only do we get the pleasure of the word play or jesting, but we also gratify forbidden impulses. Perhaps most important, we get pleasure from the psychic economy that makes the inhibition unneeded ("It's only a joke"), as in the "relief" theories of the comic.

Tendentious jokes, even though they give most of their pleasure by gratifying forbidden impulses, need innocent jesting and word play as a formal disguise. That is, only if they are disguised as word play do we allow ourselves to gratify these tendencies without anxiety. The playfulness of the joke serves as a kind of cue to relax the intellect a little and trigger the much greater relaxation of an inhibition against sex or aggression. Physical laughter embodies the free discharge of the extra energy released because the inhibition (for the moment of the joke) does not have to inhibit.

Freud's view of joking, then, is that it gives us pleasure by *an economy of psychic expenditure in inhibition.*

At least the person who is being told a joke gets that pleasure. The person who makes up the joke doesn't. In getting pleasure from a joke, three people are usually involved: the one who invents the joke, a second person against whom it is directed, and a third to whom the first tells the joke. Sometimes there is no second person, but the third is absolutely indispensable to the joke transaction. (Think of the way you feel when a joke you tell falls flat.)

The third person licenses, by his laughter, the forbidden impulse revealed by the joke's inventor. That third person, therefore, must not have heard the joke before. Otherwise he will not dam up the impulse, will have no excess energy to release—he will not laugh.

Similarly, the maker of the joke does not laugh (unless he does so vicariously), except in so far as he gets pleasure from gratifying the exhibitionistic impulse that made him "undress" his unconscious impulses in the first place. To be a jokemaker, you need to have strong impulses pressing against strong inhibitions; otherwise you will not seek sublimated satisfaction through wit. A jokester is likely to be, as Hobbes pointed out, rather insecure.

In distinguishing jokes from the comic (in a specific sense), Freud says that the comic requires only two people: one who finds (as opposed to invents) something funny, and one in whom he finds it. The comic is limited to human beings and their social relations: movements, shapes, actions, or characters. Freud explains the comic as someone's seeing a superfluous expenditure of energy and identifying with it by saying, "See how I could do the same thing with very little effort" (as when we find children's efforts ludicrous). Or "See how much effort it would take me to achieve the same effect" (as when we laugh at a clown's gymnastics).

Joking gives us pleasure by converting a conscious process full of energy and tension into an easy unconscious process. In the comic, however, we compare two conscious (or at least automatic) expenditures of energy. We see an unnecessary effort and imagine a simpler way. We compare the relative complexities of body and mind, for example, muscular energies and the ease and swiftness of thought. Or we see an expectation defeated. We unmask the important to find the common. We convert the serious to the trivial, as in caricature, parody, and travesty.

Thus Freud can answer Pascal's question (Why are twins funny?). Experience tells us that each living being is different and demands a considerable amount of effort to understand. When we see identical twins, we halve that effort, and the extra goes off as laughter.[32]

Freud calls nonsense the comic of words. He gives as examples "the comic nonsense produced by ignorant students at examinations," such as "Clio, the Medusa of history," or "For hours the battle raged; finally it remained inconclusive." Nonsense reveals nothing about unconscious processes.

Rather, our pleasure from the comic comes entirely from *an economy of expenditure in thought*. To be appreciated, both jokes and the comic ask us suddenly to compare things. The comic, however, also requires an expectation of the comic, fixed attention, freedom from strong feelings or interests, and a minimum of abstraction, so the amused person can imagine freely and graphically.

Freud's first and longer essay *Jokes and Their Relation to the Unconscious* treats humor only slightly. We find it chiefly in character situations where we expect to have to give much sympathy, but then find our sympathies not needed (Don Quixote or Falstaff, for example, or Mark Twain's brother, who while working on a road project was thrown ten miles away by an explosion—and then docked half a day's pay for being away from the job). Freud defines humor as another kind of comparison: *an economy of expenditure of emotion*.

Freud's 1905 book explains jokes in terms of the first phase of psychoanalysis: by a tension between "the" conscious and "the" unconscious. As nouns, these key terms not only describe awareness ("I wasn't conscious I was doing that") but imply systems, even locations, in the mind. Slowly, however, during the next two decades, Freud realized that he was seeing many things in his clinical work (notably expressions of unconscious guilt) that he could not explain by a simple contrast between conscious and unconscious systems.

By 1923 Freud had rethought his earlier explanation. He replaced this "topographic" model (conscious–unconscious) with a "structural" one. By "structure" he meant mental functions or forms that last a long time compared to our constantly fluctuating wishes, fears, hopes, perceptions, and memories. In this, the second phase of psychoanalysis, Freud and his followers explained events in terms not of conscious–unconscious, but of ego–nonego.

The ego he defined as an executive or synthetic function of the mind that from early infancy onward works out compromises among the inner and outer demands on us. Four other structures represent those demands: id, superego, reality, and the repetition compulsion.

By "id" he meant the mental representation of basic biological drives, sex and aggression, pressing for satisfaction. By "superego" he meant our positive aspirations toward ideals combined with moral inhibitions ("thou shalt" and "thou shalt not"). The superego forms as we identify with our parents and through them with their culture. The repetition compulsion, in its most immediate sense, means simply our tendency—the tendency of any organism—to return to ways of coping that have previously worked before we try new ones. Freud spoke of the "inertia" or "conservatism" of the instincts. Reality is the ultimate question, obviously, but in this context it means something that constantly poses new challenges and requires the ego to find new ways to meet them. It balances the compulsion to repeat (the new vs. the old) as the id counterpoises the superego (Do it! Don't do it!). The polarity ego–nonego includes but supplants the earlier polarity conscious–unconscious. Those terms become adjectives. One speaks of "conscious ego" or "unconscious superego" instead of "the" unconscious.

In a 1927 essay, "Humour," Freud adapted his earlier ideas about humor to his new second-phase, structural model, and he hinted at the way other things we laugh at would fit it. In humor, a laugher alters the usual relation between superego and ego. One spares oneself the painful emotions to which a painful situation would naturally give rise, in particular the pain of guilt. Thus "humor has in it a *liberating* element. . . . It is the triumph of narcissism, the ego's victorious assertion of its own invulnerability. It refuses to be hurt by the arrows of reality or to be compelled to suffer. It insists that it is impervious to wounds dealt by the outside world, in fact that these are merely occasions for affording it pleasure." The ego, in other words, acts like an *eiron*.

When one adopts a humorous attitude toward others, one is adopting "the attitude of an adult toward a child, recognizing and smiling at the triviality of the interests and sufferings which seem to the child so big." When one adopts a humorous attitude toward oneself, one is "removing the accent from the ego and transferring it on to his superego." As in jokes unconscious impulses circumvent the limits imposed by the ego, so in humor the superego makes the problem, big to the ego, seem suddenly very small. In a humorous attitude toward others or toward oneself, the superego takes the role of an exalted but comforting parent.

Freud's second theory of humor neatly dovetails with his structural model of the mind. Humor arises in the relation between superego and ego. A joke allows the id's impulses to thread their way through the ego's defenses. The comic becomes the ego's own comparison between two different ego processes (of thought, for example, and movement). Thus humor is to superego as comic is to ego as joke is to id. Freud's second-phase explanation does not contradict the first. Rather he has placed the first within a larger theory that explains more of human behavior.

As he said at the end of the 1905 book, all three types of the comic are ways we have of

> regaining from mental activity a pleasure which has in fact been lost through the development of that activity. For the euphoria which we endeavour to reach by these means is nothing other than the mood of a period of life in which we were accustomed to deal with our psychic work in general with a small expenditure of energy—the mood of our childhood, when we were ignorant of the comic, when we were incapable of jokes and when we had no need of humour to make us feel happy in our life.

Characteristically for Freud, laughter embodies a frontal assault on adult reality.

Many people have contested Freud's explanation because he (like Hobbes) makes the comic rather nasty.[33] Logically, however, you can't refute Freud's claim that laughter "is" this way with "It ought not to be."

A more interesting critique, that of Benedetto Croce, says that Freud enunciates characteristics that apply to "every spiritual process, such as the succession of painful and pleasing moments, and the satisfaction arising from the consciousness of strength and of its free expansion." Croce takes one of the great strengths of Freud's theory of humor and tries to turn it around: he objects to Freud's being able to relate laughter and the laughable to other psychic processes, such as dreaming and symptom formation, which we can understand more thoroughly. I don't think, though, that Freud's description of laughter actually covers other psychic events as well. Rather, it is quite precise. Indeed, what appeals to me most in Freud's theory is that one can use his theory to examine details of particular jokes and cartoons. Croce does not realize this possibility.

A more telling objection to Freud's theory is that much of it rests on the questionable concept of psychic energy, which has been falling out of favor in psychoanalytic circles since about 1960. One can, however, state the theory more in terms of structures and subsequent developments in psychoanalytic theory, ego psychology, and object relations theory (as I do in Part II).

Many psychoanalysts have added to Freud's theory without fundamentally changing its 1905 style. They have included "Freudian" symbolism in the process and the idea that the comic is "love checked by hate," hence an expression of ambivalence.[34] Ludwig Jekels pointed to an inverted oedipal triangle in comedy: in tragedy the son is guilty, in comedy the father. And quite recently theorists have expanded Freud's analysis in various nonpsychoanalytic directions: extending it from jokes to dramatic comedy; allying it with gestalt psychology and Noam Chomsky's transformational linguistics (the deep structure contains the "tendentious" wit, surface structure the word play); making it into a series of propositions that can be experimentally tested.[35]

In between, Edmund Bergler linked Freud's early theory to ego psychology in a very rich and intricate way, suggesting that jokes represent attacks by the ego on a torturing superego. He could then compare the form of particular jokes to particular complicated combinations of defense mechanisms (an early statement of the idea of "form as defense"). Sidney Tarachow developed this defensive idea by comparing the comic to art in general. The artist magically destroys feared and hated objects, but replaces them with symbols we can love. The comedian, however, simply destroys the object without providing a replacement. He thereby frees us, but he does not attain beauty. Art resolves ambivalence; the comic only disguises it.

As part of this defensive aspect of the comic, as every practicing psychiatrist or psychoanalyst knows, a patient may smile, giggle, or joke, not because he feels amused, but because he feels anxious. Conversely, the therapist may use humor either to relieve or to ward off anxiety. Not only the feeling of being amused but also the physical act of laughing can serve as a defense.[36]

Among psychoanalytic writers, no one has worked more fruitfully than Ernst Kris with Freud's second-phase, ego-psychological explanation of jokes, the comic, and humor. Kris extended Freud's analysis of verbal wit to visual caricature in order to answer the historical question: Why did caricature develop so late—not until the sixteenth century? Because thinking in images is so deeply rooted in us that we could not play with people's images until we no longer felt, deep down, that the image was the person, and that defacing the image magically caused actual harm. In true caricature, however, we sense that the image is only a likeness.[37]

In showing that visual caricature, like verbal wit, depends on such magical, dreamlike "primary process" thinking, Kris was enlarging the first-phase theory of wit in the light of Freud's second-phase, structural model of the mind. Two things, Kris notes, make it possible to evade censorship: the content satisfies the id; the disguise or form satisfies the superego. The second makes the comic highly specific to a particular time, place, or topic. The comic cannot deal, says Kris, with the eternally forbidden (murder, say) or with material to which the superego is indifferent. It must deal with something represented *now* in the superego. Hence the fashion plates of twenty-five to fifty years ago, our parents' youth, are funny. Those of two hundred years ago are not.

In general, comic phenomena seem to come from past conflicts of the ego. The comic enables us to repeat an earlier victory and once more overcome half-mastered fear. Therefore people can enjoy the comic only when they feel completely secure from danger. Hence to laugh, one needs detachment or distance. Identification with the person laughed at spoils the fun. In this sense, again, the comic is a mode of defense, serving to master and ward off anxiety.

Finally Kris applied ego psychology to physical laughter. In one sense, laughter is a way of making contact with other people in the environment; hence it is purposeful. But laughter is also the sign of a feeling. Hence laughter occurs on the borderline between purposeful (ego-controlled) behavior and expressive (id-dominated) behavior. Like other artistic phenomena, laughter and the comic engage us in *a regression in the service of the ego*. That is, we return to more childish aims or modes of thought, not in a pathological way, but as a first step in creativity and renewal. A smile suggests that the ego has won control, while laughter reveals either the weakening of the ego, as by the presence of other people who are laughing, or the strengthening of the drives, as by anger at the butt of a joke. Shades of Lord Chesterfield.

Laughter, Kris notes, involves much the same physiological processes no matter what its tone: ironic, hilarious, teasing, whatever. He suggests that it is, as it were, a mechanism prepared in advance. The ego shapes and tones the one basic physical act to achieve the remarkable range of communication of which our facial expressions are capable. From this point of view, laughter, like all expressions of feeling, is a function of the ego as well as of the id.

In another major psychoanalytic development after Freud, psychoanalysts began to study children's laughter. Edith Jacobson concluded that a child can laugh as it feels free enough to play with an achievement of the ego (as Kris says). A child can also laugh because of temporary ego support from a group of other children who are giggling. And a child can laugh from the mere simulation of an ego achievement so long as it allows the child to feel superior to someone (parents or itself earlier).

Martha Wolfenstein observed that as children develop they progressively incorporate inhibitions against the simple expression of impulses. Jokes are one of the devices they master to get around those same inhibitions. (Again the comic as defense.)

The work of René Spitz, beginning in the 1940s, brought a new sophistication to our understanding of the first smiling and laughing. In the 1920s research consisted mostly of descriptions of children's behavior, beginning with the basic fact that the child has usually begun to smile and to laugh in a general way by the age of four months. The experts speak of "the unspecific, social smile."[38] Spitz confirmed that the specific smiling response, directed to the mother, appears around the third month of life: it is rare to find it before then, and rare not to find it after the fifth month. There is something special about that time, moreover. The smile comes at a time when the infant shifts from passivity to directed activity in other spheres. The smiling response thus marks the beginning of our earliest thought processes. It is the infant's sign, says Spitz, for "expected need gratification." If the baby can *expect*, then the baby has been able to establish memory traces of the hoped-for gratification.

Such memory traces are a prerequisite for recognitions of all kinds. When they are evident, the infant has progressed beyond total absorption in self (primary narcissism) to be able to imagine, in a limited way, another person. In psychoanalytic jargon, the infant can relate to a "preobject." That is, the child does not perceive and respond to another person as such (an "object"), but to certain specific signs of another person: the combination, in motion, of forehead, nose, and eyes (and two eyes; just one will not do). If all four signs are present, no matter how grotesque their form, a baby will smile. Lacking any one sign, it will not. A baby will smile at a nodding Halloween mask but not at a human profile. Interestingly, the infant will smile more readily and reliably if one replaces a smile on the nodding face of the observer "by extreme widening of the mouth, somewhat after the manner of a savage animal baring its fangs." What dark vestige of our hominid past can *that* be?

Whatever it is, the smiling response does seem to take us back into our primate history. So far as human infants are concerned, it constitutes a cluster of muscular behavior (like laughter itself), an "ego nucleus" that is in its essentials programmed and autonomous from birth. As such it plays an important part in the bodily dialogue between mother and child. Later it will wane, as the eight-month-old child values different faces differently and therefore shows either anxiety at strangers or a more chosen smile for loved adults. Yet it seems entirely possible that the early function of the smile as the sign of "expected need gratification" may provide a meaning for smiling and laughter all through life.

While American psychoanalytic theorists worked on form and children's laughter, Charles Mauron, one of the most brilliant of the French psychoanalytic critics, returned to content. He developed a method of studying literature which he called *psychocritique*. By, as it were, superimposing on one another all the writings by a given author, he could point to recurring patterns that constituted a "personal myth."

In 1964 he applied this technique not to an individual, but to the whole genre of comedy, and concluded that two basic fantasies underlie all comedies. First, "comic art is founded on a triumphal game—originally the restoration of the lost mother." Her disappearance and return form the up and down of the basic comic pattern. The energy with which the child yearns when she is absent goes into a feeling of richness, of surplus, when she returns. This fantasy underlies comic writing all through human history.

A second fantasy becomes progressively more important as one traces comedy from Aristophanes to Molière: the old man baffled, which becomes the theme of cuckoldry (the oedipal issue so many writers have noted). Mauron's theory ties adult comedy, then, to the two major crises in the personal relationships of the developing child: psychological separation from a mother and rivalry with a father.

Since Kris and Mauron, psychoanalysis has developed a number of new psychological ideas that may shed light on the comic. For example, the so-called English school has explored in considerable clinical detail the early relationship of baby and "primary caretaker" (mother, usually) and the way the child forms itself by compliance with the other who is "there." The integrity of a self grows from "object constancy" (psychoanalytic jargon for the child's ability to think of, to expect, and to trust in a sometimes absent other). The English thus offer us a way of talking about the "menace" or "incongruity" of the comic as a limited threat to the wholeness of the ego we so painfully and triumphantly consolidated in childhood. The comic plays with object constancy and with the wholeness of ourselves. Mauron touches on these matters, but newer theory allows still more. We shall return in Chapter 11 to "the joke as other."

Otto Kernberg in the United States has studied the child's development of an ego by incorporating and identifying with parents and significant others. It seems to me that Kernberg makes it possible to consider jokes and comic writing as a drama within the laugher among the representatives of significant early others. After all, jokes give us horseplay with father and mother figures, rivals (analogous to sibs), judges and doctors (modeled after parents), and the like. Further, Kernberg's distinction between the defense of splitting and the less unhealthy defense of repression can be related to different kinds of incongruities. And there are probably other ways of using his theories to study jokes as intrapsychic dramas.

Heinz Lichtenstein, also in the United States, has developed theories of personal style and identity as they grow in the early relation of baby and "primary caretaker." He gives us a way to approach the individuality of a particular, personal sense of humor—but more of that in Part II.

In France, Jacques Lacan has related child development to the network of language—signifiers (loosely, words) and signifieds (loosely, meanings)—provided to the infant by mother, father, and culture. Here again the theory seems obviously applicable to the comic. Incongruity—Koestler's trains of association—for example, corresponds to leaps and short circuits among Lacan's shifting and insisting signifiers. Further, an individual's associations, his characteristic paths through his linguistic network, let us talk about his particular sense of humor.

In the United States, Heinz Kohut has proposed a "psychology of the self," tracing a line of development parallel to the traditional Freudian sequence of oral, anal, phallic, and oedipal. The child who at first knows no boundary between itself and the world transforms that first feeling of omnipotence into grandiose or idealized images of its parents, from which in turn it builds its own psychic structures. By finding an origin for feelings of grandiosity or the ideal, Kohut offers ways of talking in great detail about the "superiority" or "sudden glory" of Hobbes's theory and the fragmentation involved in the deflation of an ideal or "incongruity" in general. Like Lacan, he seems to offer a dual way of talking about the funny: both as external stimuli (the incongruities of Chapter 1) and as the individual's shaping of those stimuli to a personal sense of humor.

In short, the last couple of decades have seen a flurry of developments in psychoanalytic theory which open all kinds of new avenues for exploring aspects of the comic. So far as I know, however, no psychoanalytic writers have prowled them yet.

Experimental Psychology

All arts, it is said, aspire to the condition of music. Psychoanalysis, for instance, may be a duet improvised between a piccolo and a tuba. Experimental psychology must be trying to be the metronome. Where psychoanalytic theories of humor value the possibilities and variabilities of a joke, experimentalists prize the ability to count—but right away they meet a problem.

Basically, there are two approaches.[39] You can measure the intensity of a person's actual physical laughing, or you can try to measure a person's feeling that "this is funny." Asking people how they feel is easy but unreliable. Measuring laughter is reliable, but are you really then measuring humor?

For example, one experimenter decided whether members of a group were witty or not on the basis of the "Observer Wit Tally." Whenever some member of the group "said or did anything which resulted in an audible laughter-type response [sic] on the part of at least two other group members, the monitoring observer (*O*) was instructed to credit that member with a witticism." Scientific as all this sounds, doesn't a joke that everybody laughs at count for more than a joke that two people go *heh-heh* to? And does a *heh-heh* count as much as a belly laugh? And then, as other researchers point out, we laugh at a joke, but we also laugh just to be convivial, or to hide our failure to get a joke, or to ridicule somebody, or because we feel anxious or apologetic or joyful or embarrassed or ignorant—or because somebody tickles us.[40]

You can, of course, measure how long a person laughs and how loud, for example, on a scale of o ("no response") to 4 ("audible laughter"). You can refine that measurement by timing voice onset and offset and gauging the total speech pressure wave. You can use a "laryngograph" to measure "intonation contour" (whether a person is going *ho-ho-ho* or *tee-hee-hee*).[41] But what are you measuring? To be sure, being doubled over argues more amusement than a thin smile. But does a two-second titter mean twice as much hilarity as a one-second guffaw? Does a loud *haw-haw* mean the person *feels* the joke is ten decibels funnier than someone who laughs a tiny *hee-hee*?

The alternative (and most experimenters take it) is a "humor rating." The experimenter asks the subject to report whether this joke is funnier than that, to arrange cartoons in order of funniness, to rank comedians on a scale of 1 to 10, and so on. Unfortunately, this method involves all the uncertainties of introspection, and there seems to be no way of coping with the possibility that one person's 8 is "the same as" another person's 4.

Common sense would suggest combining the two, and some psychologists do, even though the one experiment that investigated correspondences between the two measures seems to be inconclusive.[42]

Despite the difficulty in measuring, a great many psychologists have dug into the topic of humor in the last dozen years or so. The literature has become enormous, to the point where the very summaries of all this work are too long to summarize. The most recent "big" book in the field contains 96 articles and a bibliography of 1,135 items.[43]

Further, much of this literature is written in a strange dialect: "Experiments now in progress hope to establish whether fewer than three dimensions of value normative anticonformity suffice to generate incongruity humour, and whether the minimum number of required dimensions anticonformed to depends upon if the norms violated represent ego-involving values or non-ego-involving beliefs."

Given such problems of bulk and translation, I can do no more here than sketch trends and issues.[44] The issue that interests me most in this mass of research is this: A given joke is the same for everybody, but the responses vary widely. How can we account both for the variation and for what uniformity there is? In exploring this question, psychologists have adopted two styles. I call them Huck Finn and the Great White Hunter.

A Huck Finn follows the bent-pin school of fishing. The psychologist chooses some jokes, picks some people to be subjects, and writes down who finds what how funny. Then he uses some of the astonishing statistical methods made possible by modern calculators and computers to try to connect factors in the stimuli with factors in the persons.

Some studies try to relate aspects of humor to very general variables, such as age and sex. Others use differences in response to explore the sources of humor and the ways we understand it. And still others try to link different facets of humor with different traits of personality.

For general variables, the experimenters' conclusions have that helter-skelter look which such haphazard searches for correlations get. For example, the funnier a subject thought a cartoon to be, the more the pupils of his eyes would dilate. Other researchers have found correlations between joke preferences and height or traffic violations. You see? Height as a measure of "superiority" and speeding as a measure of aggression. Still other researchers found that women who were dieting were less influenced by the laughter of others in an audience than women who were not dieting. (Would I had space to spell out the logic that makes *that* correlation important.)[45]

The second group of Huck Finn studies, those that use individual differences in response to explore aspects of humor or the way we process humor, have confirmed some traditional categories: hostile humor, impudent humor, humor involving immortality or transcendence, sexual humor, and so on. For example, one line of research has demonstrated that if a joke disparages a positive IC ("the joke recipient's identification class") or if it esteems a negative IC, the joke will not be perceived as amusing. If, however, a joke esteems a positive IC or disparages a negative IC, the "recipient" will find it funny.

The conclusion one group of researchers reaches is that research is shifting Hobbes's original superiority theory toward vicarious superiority and heightened *self*-esteem, so that one can conclude, "Necessary ingredients of an adequate theory of humour would seem to involve a (1) *sudden* (2) *happiness increment* . . . as a consequence of a (3) *perceived incongruity*." But isn't this just combining some by now quite familiar theories and variations on theories? Have we really gotten much farther than Hobbes's "sudden glory"?[46]

The third strategy, linking types of joke to traits in the hearer, seems more promising, but the results are less clear. One experimenter found that men prefer jokes that express hostility directly while women prefer subtle verbal hostility, especially against men. An earlier experimenter, however, found no significant difference between male and female senses of humor. One early study found that strong responses to aggressive, disparaging jokes went with a generally aggressive personality. Another study showed that mental patients who could empathize could also recognize "funniness." Yet another found that extroverts prefer simple and sexual jokes (laughter based on a consciousness of superior adaptation) and introverts prefer complex and nonsexual jokes (laughter stemming from sudden, insightful integration of incongruous ideas, suitably distanced).[47]

One psychologist used factor analysis of responses to subdivide Freud's single category "humor" into subtypes, such as "loss of face" and "being pursued." A more elaborate factor analysis of 100 jokes and people's responses to them yielded clusters of apparently related jokes and responses that could be described by such factors as "good-natured self-assertion," "rebellious dominance," "easygoing sensuality," and so on. The researchers decided that these were not just joke types but general personality factors, and concluded that people prefer jokes that are like themselves.[48] Vague as these studies may be, I find the conclusion that people use jokes to mirror themselves both interesting and probable.

Further, these correlations of joke themes with character traits lead, obviously, to an intriguing inversion—studies not about humor as such, but about people. Does one's sense of humor reveal one's personality? Once experimenters could link particular personality traits to laughing at particular jokes, the next step was obvious: the use of jokes to discover traits. Thus were born WHAT, MRT, and the IPAT Humor Test of Personality: the Wit and Humor Appreciation Test, the Mirth Response Test, and the Institute for Personality and Ability Testing Humor Test of Personality.[49]

The two humor tests work with joke preferences among three of Freud's types—humor, hostile jokes, and jests—to assess personality types. The Mirth Response Test follows a later psychoanalytic model: jokes express conflict-ridden wishes in conditions that avert anxiety. If a joke is either conflict-free or overconflicted for a given person, he or she will not laugh. In particular, if the theme of the joke is too "hot," the person may either block perception of a crucial part of the joke (denial) or distort it by projecting some private motive onto the originator. For example, the Mirth Response Test used James Thurber's well-known cartoon "Home." One subject, shown the cartoon,

HOME

"failed to see the face, despite hints and prodding, until it was actually traced out for her. Then she was not amused but upset." The Mirth Response Testers concluded that their subject could not read the drawing of "a very small and frightened man coming home to a house which takes the form of the large angry face of a woman waiting threateningly for his entrance" (note how their phrasings imply their own interpretation). She could not see the woman's face because she "had extremely hostile and competitive feelings toward men which she found difficult to control." Her denial of the woman in the cartoon enabled her "to avoid the conflict that was so distressing to her." Her failure to laugh thus fitted into general principles about humans' defenses against painful conflict.

The same group of experimenters showed Charles Addams' cartoon of his macabre "Addams family" on the tower of their eerie Victorian mansion while a cluster of innocent Christmas carolers sing at their front door. The Addams family is just tipping a cauldron of boiling oil on them.

One woman found this cartoon particularly funny. She had rejected her religious upbringing, and for her the cartoon represented "emancipation from the repression of her youth." A young man, however, found the cartoon pointless and disgusting. He, too, had left the church in which he had been active, but "the cartoon brought out his conflict and his feeling of guilt." Again, laughing or not laughing relates to a general strategy for avoiding conflict.[50] Unfortunately, in later papers the Mirth Response Testers retreated from this sophisticated model and its promising line of research toward simply relating joke preferences to diagnostic categories.

These odd responses in lieu of amusement are not elicited just by psychoanalytically inclined experimenters. H. J. Eysenck, a vehement experimentalist, reports a woman's response to a cartoon showing a witch in full Halloween regalia, pointed hat and all, flying along on a vacuum cleaner. The cartoon was funny, she said, because the price indicated on the tag attached to the vacuum cleaner was too low.[51] To me, such responses suggest that we ought to investigate individual, even idiosyncratic, laughings, but they evidently do not say the same to experimental psychologists. Both Huck Finns and Great White Hunters demand categories that submerge individuality in a class.

The Great White Hunter is the experimenter who comes to the study of people's responses to jokes equipped with all the latest thinking about personality: social-psychological theory, cognitive theory, theory of affect (emotion), alone or in combination. They do overlap, of course, since personality develops in a society as a result of skills and feelings.

Theories of society and culture touch on humor in several ways. For one, they show how people choose certain subjects for joking. Jews tell Jewish jokes. Soldiers joke about death and army food. Hospital patients tell jokes about being flat on one's back. Americans' jokes are apparently more aggressive than those of other nationalities. On social occasions, men start the joking whether or not women are present. Women don't.

Different cultures choose different subjects for jokes. The Chinese joke about social relationships. Nonliterate cultures joke about the immediate physical environment. The West jokes about sex and aggression. But at a more abstract level, all cultures show a structure of incongruity and resolution, perhaps demonstrating Franz Boas' idea of a primitive mind in all of us or Claude Lévi-Strauss's theory that all humanity builds on a bipolar, oppositional structure of mind.[52]

Social theories also point to certain contexts for jokes: a night club, a banquet (the after-dinner speaker), a wedding breakfast. They may indicate the accepted forms for jokes: "There was a Scotchman, an Irishman, and a Jew . . ." "How many Californians does it take to change a light bulb?" Such theories also discuss the complex balance of group closeness and distance required for joking.

At the same time, however, one should not expect much certainty from these social-psychological theories. The evidence as to the homogeneity of, for example, audience laughter at a comedy is mixed. Some psychologists find high uniformity, others don't, and the evidence from producers and directors is equally mixed. One factor does seem to count consistently: the smaller the audience, the fewer the laughs.[53] Otherwise, the response seems as unpredictable as for the philosophers, literary critics, and psychoanalysts.

Similarly, those who study responses of audiences to such popular comedians as Bill Cosby, Phyllis Diller, and Don Rickles find the variability striking. Jokes that the professors find funny fail with the student subjects of their experiments. Jokes that get guffaws at an 8:00 P.M. showing of a movie bomb at 10:00, and vice versa. An audience of people already friendly to one another laughs more than an audience of strangers (at least in a laboratory setting). Student "plants" in the audience (instructed either to over- or to underlaugh) affect group responses "enormously." "The major point seems to be that what's funny is not simply a consequence of comic material. Rather, the nature of the audience and the comedian's personal style all combine with one another to produce a given effect."[54] Social psychologists have their work cut out for them.

Cognitive personality theory guides humor research into another large set of inquiries. To be funny, a joke must be neither too simple nor too hard to understand. Hence an important supplement to the experiments correlating traits with jokes are developmental studies that trace changes in what children laugh at—and these changes, too, are very numerous—to judge from the surveys.[55]

The physical acts of laughing and smiling do not change, but the number of situations that provoke them rapidly increases during the first years of life. It is as though our ability to laugh, like our ability to speak, is innate, but we learn our particular culture's way of doing it. In our society, the boisterous, shouting laughter of the child gives way to a more adult sense of the incongruous or a feeling of irresponsibility (like the child again).[56]

Laughter first appears in the fourth month of life, and once it has appeared, the stimuli that become more and more effective are those that make the most cognitive demands on the infant. At first there is the combination of "stimulus-maintaining" and "stimulus-termination" tendencies (as in tickling or coochy-coo). Later laughter signals success in meeting cognitive demands. For the two- or three-year-old, "laughter and probably smiling may be considered as socially acceptable tics or compensatory motor mechanisms accompanying the resolution of conflicts that have, for a shorter or longer period, kept the individual on the horns of a dilemma." Laughter, since it is general-within-the-species behavior, must be adaptive. Perhaps it may reinforce our ability to deal with new and incongruous situations.[57]

In general, say these theories of cognition, a child or adult has to be able to "process" the joke. You have to get the right "set" or expectation. You have to be able to detect an incongruity (and, of course, the joke has to present you with a whole that is also incongruous). You have to be able to tolerate the incongruity, to find it "safe." The person who tickles the baby has to be a familiar person. The comedian's audience has to feel friendly. To laugh, you need to be free of anxiety. The joke can't hurt someone you love. You need to know it is "all in fun."[58] In short, cognitive psychologists' studies of humor support the traditional requirement of "play" (described in Chapter 3).

The most challenging and extensive work on humor from the Great White Hunters has combined theories of cognition with theories of emotion, and in this mode the work of D. E. Berlyne on "arousal" bulks large. We experience something positively or negatively as our arousal fluctuates. Moderate levels of novelty or incongruity lead to an arousal "boost" and positive feelings. Low or very high levels of arousal lead to negative feelings, but a rise to an uncomfortably high level of arousal followed by a fall is an arousal "jag" and leads to pleasure. These quantities can overlap so that we can even have an "arousal boost-jag." And something can become pleasurable just because we associate it with an arousal jag.

Berlyne relates the pleasure of a joke to these fluctuations in the level of our arousal and hence to the way we know the joke, its "cognitive aspects." Three characteristics of a joke lead to arousal. First, such psychophysical properties as size, shape, frequency, and duration play minor roles. Second, "ecological properties" build on the pleasant or harmful experience a subject has had with the materials of the joke. Third, our arousal varies according to the way we process "collative properties" of the joke. That is, the way we compare or collate information from two or more sources allows us to arrive in a certain way at the surprise or novelty or redundancy or uncertainty or complexity of the joke. These three kinds of properties have to lead to an optimal arousal or an "arousal jag" for the joke to get a laugh.[59]

Obviously Berlyne's "collative" factors come close to what most theorists of humor call "incongruity" and its "resolution." One psychologist, for example, discovers two stages in "getting" a joke: first, you find your expectations "disconfirmed"; second, you find some sort of rule that will make the punch line follow from the body of the joke—that will, in other words, resolve the incongruity. Naturally, the resolution can give rise to a further incongruity (as in a comedian's string of gags), but the psychologists also remark that "even distinguishing resolution from incongruity is difficult."[60]

To muddy the waters further, other psychological research suggests that the perception of incongruity alone, without any resolution, is enough to make us laugh. Sophomores laughed when they picked up weights that were markedly lighter or heavier than they had expected them to be—but then sophomores will laugh at a lot of strange things. So also children as old as eleven or twelve preferred jokes with just incongruity, no resolution.[61]

One research team suggests a "theory of psychological reversals" to improve these arousal and incongruity-recognition theories. In our ordinary "telic" state, we choose to get onto a bicycle to ride to a restaurant to eat. We choose behaviors leading to goals. In a "paratelic" state we bicycle because we enjoy bicycling. We choose a goal to support a behavior we enjoy for its own sake. We laugh because we are feeling hilarious already. We are either in a telic, purposeful state or in a paratelic state, never both. If we are telic, a high level of arousal makes us feel anxious, a low level relaxes us. If we are in a paratelic state, a high level of arousal becomes excitement and a low level boredom. Now think about synergy: two cognitive opposites come together so that each enhances the other. A man drinking champagne on Skid Row looks better off than he does drinking champagne on Park Avenue, and the champagne makes the Sterno drunk on Skid Row look even worse. Synergies in the telic state arouse and so displease; in the paratelic state, they arouse and so please.

Now, equipped in true White Hunter style, we can explain humor. A person feels humor when (1) he is in a paratelic state, (2) a synergy occurs involving two aspects of one situation, and (3) it is sudden. Now that seems to me rather like two old favorites: incongruity plus play (lack of purpose); but this theory's advocates claim it is an arousal theory superior to Berlyne's because it allows for two preferred levels: the individual goes back and forth between telic and paratelic states. It is the opposite of the relief theories (see above, pp. 43–44), because arousal, not relief, makes us laugh, but it is, of course, another incongruity theory.[62]

In having two levels, it resembles another complicated theory put forward not by a psychologist, but by a mathematician. John Paulos suggests that laughter is one of a number of phenomena that answer to the "catastrophe theory" of René Thom: a three-dimensional mathematical curve (combining a saddle, a cusp, and a discontinuity) which describes situations of abrupt, discontinuous change, such as a dog's moving from snarling fear to barking anger, lightning flashing, a car lurching, a person going crazy—such as laughing. Like the psychologists' "theory of reversal," this is incongruity writ large through mathematics.

A further complication: "Any incongruity-resolution analysis of humour is problematic," writes a reviewer of the field, "in that, given current formulations, we cannot distinguish the process of humour appreciation from the process of problem-solving,"[63] especially the feeling of exuberance and triumph that goes with mastery. Hence some psychologists try to make the emotional side of humor more precise. "How can the combination of arousal with cognition lead to the distinctive subjective experience of humour and joy?" ask two theorists of affect.[64] They answer that each emotion can be thought of as distinct, unique, and self-evident. Arousal and cognition together make us laugh *if* they occur within the feeling that goes with smiling and laughing. In other words, they argue, laughter involves a complicated feedback. We feel like laughing (for whatever reason). The right stimulus occurs—a witch riding a vacuum cleaner, say—and we do laugh. The laughing is a sign that we have "processed" the joke within an "emotion category." This is the reason, they say, we can laugh at something we wouldn't ordinarily find funny just because we are feeling silly.

The idea that we have distinct "emotion categories" seems to me to carry to an extreme one of the difficulties I have with all these experimental approaches. They gather a whole sequence of events (each separate and distinct: different cartoons, different people, different laughings) and homogenize them into one class, category, factor, or trait. Then they start comparing, counting, or factoring the homogenized class. That feels to me like trying to cut, slice, and count applesauce as though it were still apples.

A notable exception comes from a husband-and-wife team. Prompted by their clinical work with intractable *schlemiel* children, Seymour and Rhoda Fisher decided to investigate what makes a child try to be a comic—and succeed. They interviewed professional clowns and comedians, gave them projective tests (notably Rorschach inkblots), and collected published autobiographical accounts. Then they counted the relative frequencies with which certain themes appeared in the comedians' phrasings of their tests and in their autobiographies.

The Fishers insist they have not been able to isolate a "comic personality" as such, and they doubt that anyone will ever draw a neat "trait profile" of the professional comedian. They did, however, establish "focalized areas of tension and doubt" shared to a remarkable degree by comedians and not by other, related types. (Their controls were professional actors and performers, nonprofessional "funny friends," and ministers and priests.)

The "most salient theme" had to do with contrasts and opposites. The comedian presents himself as reassuringly silly, yet he conjures up the most taboo subjects. He is superfriendly, but he assails one and all with disparaging remarks. He wants his audience to love him, yet comics say they get a feeling of power over their audiences. In the inkblot tests, the Fishers got a "highly unique 'nice monster' imagery." The comedian would describe an inkblot figure as a dragon or a hyena but a few minutes later turn it into a cuddly or misunderstood pet. Bad things aren't really bad.

In general, comics wrestled with such questions as "Is the world good or bad?" "Am I good or bad?" And they would define themselves and others first in one direction, then the other.

When the Fishers asked about childhood, they found that comics generally saw their mothers as disapproving and punishing and their fathers as great guys. From their mothers the comics got a message that the child was on its own, and its own was likely to be pretty poor. The child learned low self-esteem. The fathers tended to be nice but passive.

In other words, say the Fishers, the budding comedian first finds contradiction in his parents. The world is not a very predictable or logical place. In the way of children, then, the child mirrors this contradiction back to the parents, becoming himself incongruous and double, seemingly clumsy, a *schlemiel*, but actually winning from others the esteem and nurture his mother has denied him. He not only expects illogicality, he promotes it.

He begins to interpret the world as having something hidden. "There is a little lie in everything," said one comedian, and it is his business to bring it out and master it. As part of the hiddenness, the comic hides behind his own jokes, evading direct contact with others. Even so, comics tended to describe themselves as healers, in language appropriate to a physician or a priest. And society treats the comedian as double: a low-status clown who has priestlike magical powers. Robin Williams and Woody Allen have the same functions as the court jester and the fool-priest did for their cultures, and we have the same ambivalence toward them. We tend to think of even big, rich, successful comedians as petty, ridiculous figures.

At every turn the Fishers encountered the problem of size: in the inkblot responses, in the language of comic performance, in the imagery of the comics' autobiographies, in the comedian's sense that he makes himself small in order to gain power over his big audience. In a thousand ways the comic says, "I am small. I am down." Think of Woody Allen on his childhood: "I wanted a dog but my parents were too poor to buy one, so they got me an ant. I called him Spot." Or all the pratfalls in a Keystone Kops comedy.

The Fishers suggest that some combination of these "energizers of humor production are, in mirror-image fashion, represented in the mechanisms of response to humor." "It does not seem farfetched that there may be a fit between his [the professional comic's] aims and the 'humor receptors' of those who respond to him." They list, as possible features of the funny:

> Being unthreatening; soothing and healing people.
> Attacking standards, creating anarchy, blurring good
>   and bad.
> Exposing and integrating contradictions.
> Venting hostility but concealing it.
> Deprecating the self, but occupying a unique status
>   with special powers.

I see the Fishers' work as an outstanding success. They show that it is possible to count without losing sight of the individual. One can go back and forth from case to category rather than insisting, like most psychoanalysts, on only the case or, like many experimentalists, on only the category.

The difficulties I see in most other experimental results say to me that the psychologists need to be able to deal with the individual laugher *as an individual*.[65] The counting and categories most experimentalists use, however, systematically distance precisely the individuality they should be seeking. It's like reaching for a quarter that has slid down between the sofa cushions: the nearer your fingers get, the farther apart you spread the cushions, and the deeper the quarter goes.

The more you try to be "scientific" (as that is defined by most experimental psychologists), the more you have to submerge the individuality you need to understand into a "trait," a "factor," or an "index."

Yet has this effort to be scientific succeeded? To me the most basic characteristic of a science is answers: large principles that enable us to understand many situations. I do not feel that experimental psychologists who have studied humor and laughter have yet arrived at such principles. Neither do they, to judge from the psychologists who survey the field.[66]

The difficulty comes about because the answers the experimentalists do get are locked into the particular theory or method they bring to the experiment. They resist generalizing. Yet to be "scientific" (as the word is usually defined), one needs a defined, repeatable method. Perhaps, then, the real problem is not laughter, but finding a defined, repeatable method that will not smooth out the variety of response.

The writer and filmmaker Marcel Pagnol (in asserting that we laugh out of a sense of superiority) remarked, "There are no sources of the comic in nature; the source of the comic is in the One Who Laughs." "Tell me what you laugh at, and I will tell you who you are."[67] Or you could say, "Comedy is in the eye of the beholder." Carlyle provided the necessary German authority for this formula: "Every man, says Lessing, has his own style, like his own nose." I wish experimenters would pay more attention to the styles and noses that make each of us different from every other, but "scientific" psychology has not yet devised a way to take them into account.

5 *Physiology*

Philosophers and psychologists address arousals and incongruities, but finally laughter is a bodily thing. It has a purely physiological existence, separate from any psychological sense of amusement, triumph, relief, or gratification.

As a muscular phenomenon, laughter is easy to describe. It consists of spasmodic contractions of the large and small zygomatic (facial) muscles and sudden relaxations of the diaphragm accompanied by contractions of the larynx and epiglottis. Laughter differs from smiling simply in that the smile does not interrupt breathing.[1]

Experiments with electric stimuli show that laughter is reflexoid, governed by the "old brain" or "interbrain" (the thalamus and hypothalamus), along with other reflex activity and purely emotional behavior (rage, for example). It differs, therefore, from the cognitive faculties, which the pallial cortex controls.[2]

Laughter can also result from physical stimuli such as tickling or nitrous oxide (laughing gas). Certain diseases cause laughter, sometimes quite uncontrollable giggling: Kleine-Levine syndrome, Alzheimer's disease, Pick's brain atrophy, pseudobulbar palsy, multi-infarct dementia, multiple sclerosis, hebephrenic schizophrenia. Kuru, a virus disorder of New Guinea, involving the cerebellum, can lead to laughter in its terminal stages. In the rather rare gelastic epilepsy, electrical overactivity in the left hemisphere makes people laugh without intention or cause. There have even been epidemics of laugh-

ter. In 1962–64 in Uganda and Tanganyika, young girls suf-
fered from uncontrollable peals of laughter leading to exhaus-
tion.[3]

Electric stimuli can cause laughter. Indeed, one assiduous
researcher has gone so far as to produce a set of mildly enter-
taining photographs in which one half of the subject's face is
twitched into a smile by electrodes while the other half looks
thoroughly annoyed at the whole procedure.[4]

The best premodern treatise on the physiology of laughter I
have found was published in 1579 by Laurent Joubert, physician to Catherine de' Medici and Henri III. Here is his total
definition of the phenomenon:

> Laughter is a movement caused by the jubilant mind and the
> unequal agitation of the heart, which draws back the mouth and
> the lips, and shakes the diaphragm and the pectoral parts with
> impetuosity and broken-up sound, through all of which is ex-
> pressed a feeling over an ugly thing unworthy of pity. By these
> words I adequately embrace (unless I am mistaken) the whole of
> the nature of laughter.

What optimism! Truly a Renaissance man.

Joubert does not care greatly about the psychological causes
of laughter. We see something that should cause us displea-
sure, and it doesn't. Therefore we feel a double emotion, a joy
canceled by sadness. Physiologically,

> the heart, moved impetuously in alternating contrariety, shakes
> its sheath, called the pericardium. This latter does not fail to pull
> abruptly on the diaphragm, to which it is connected with a
> strong membrane. The vacillating and trembling diaphragm in
> turn shakes the chest, following which there is a similar com-
> pression of the lungs, which breaks up the voice.

Joubert reports that when he dissected animals, he found no
connection like that in humans between the pericardium and
the diaphragm, and that, he concludes, is why humans laugh
but animals don't.

Writing not long after Rabelais, Joubert is the only author in the hundreds I have read who addresses the question "Whence it comes that one pisses, shits, and sweats by dint of laughing." As for sweating, "it is caused by the agitation and general commotion, which excite the humors and dilate the pores of the skin." As for the others, "when these [epigastric] muscles press a long time and with much violence, soliciting the bowels and the bladder to give up their contents (as it happens in laughter), if there is a quantity of liquid matter, all escapes us indecorously. For the agitation and jouncing is so strong that the sphincters are unable to resist. . . ."

Less colorful but more informative is the best modern physiological study of laughter I have found, that by Dr. Frederick R. Stearns. Laughing involves the cricothyroid and thyroartenoid muscles of the larynx in its voicing and, in its expulsion of air, the whole system of expiratory muscles: abdominal, lumbar, internal intercostal, subcostal, and transverse thoracic. The rhythmic quality of laughter, he suggests (as Bateson does), may indicate a reverberation through some neuronic feedback network. (Joubert could have said almost as much.)

What particularly intrigues Stearns is the genetic basis for this complex of muscular activity. He points out that laughter appears in all normal children of every race and culture about the fourth month of life. It must therefore be an inherited capability (like bipedal gait or, perhaps, language). Because it is made out of so many muscular actions, a series of genes or alleles (forms of a gene) must be involved. The trait, moreover, has complete "penetrance." That is, the genetic potentiality under environmental influence produces the same effect in everybody. Either we can laugh or we can't—there is no such thing as being able only to half-laugh. Moreover, the ability to laugh is not something like blue eyes or brown skin—*everybody* has it.

Knowing that laughter is an inherited potentiality, however, only makes the already perplexing physiological question more difficult: Why does a fairly specific intellectual stimulus lead to a complex cluster of muscular actions that can also be induced by various physiological means? It is as if paradoxes caused us to inhale deeply or ambiguity made us clench our fists.

Theorists have offered two answers. First, the bodily activity is an analogue to what goes on in the mind, so that we can reason backward from the physical effect or the physical cause to the mental cause. Second, laughter is a vestige of something that once had (or may still have) an important biological or adaptive function.

Laughter as Mirroring

Aristotle was a theorist of the first type. He said that people laugh when they are tickled because the "motion" (we would say stimulus) quickly penetrates to the diaphragm and there produces a movement that is independent of the will but which we nevertheless recognize intellectually. In effect, he was tracing energy from the body to the mind and vice versa.

In 1561 the Abbé Domascère outdid Aristotle by correlating a person's physical manner of laughing with personality. *Hi-hi-hi* laughs (he said) signify a melancholic personality, *hee-hee-hee* a phlegmatic one, *ho-ho-ho* (the Santa sound) a sanguine one, and (I'm guessing now) a nasty *ha-ha-ha* would mean a choleric person.[5]

René Descartes stated this linkage of body and mind most exactly. In his somewhat quaint physiology, he interpreted laughter as blood coming from the right cavity of the heart through the pulmonary artery and inflating the lungs, driving the air out of them, and so contracting the muscles of the diaphragm, chest, and throat, which in turn move the facial muscles to which they are connected. He noted that laughter often accompanies joy—but only moderate joy. "In great joys, the lung is constantly so full of blood, that it cannot be further inflated by repeated effort."

He gave two basic causes for laughter. One is physiological: "the mixture of some fluid which augments the rarefaction of the blood." The other is mental: "the Joy one has from seeing that one will not be hurt by an evil which one does not merit and by which one had been surprised by its novelty or unexpected appearance." Thus laughter will come from combinations of admiration, indignation, joy, and aversion.

A number of subsequent theorists took the same tack as Descartes. Kant, for example, started by assuming that "with all our thoughts is harmonically combined a movement in the organs of the body." Then, if we think of the mind as being transposed now to one standpoint, now to another, there will correspond "an alternating tension and relaxation of our intestines which communicates itself to the diaphragm (like that ticklish people feel)." Then the lungs will expel the air in rapidly succeeding intervals "and thus bring about a movement beneficial to health."

Similarly, Hazlitt spoke of "this alternate excitement and relaxation of the imagination" which "causes that alternate excitement and relaxation, or irregular convulsive movement of the muscular and nervous system, which constitutes physical laughter."

In our own time, Arthur Koestler attributes the laughable to "the sudden bisociation of a mental event with two habitually incompatible matrixes [which] results in an abrupt transfer of the train of thought from one associative context to another. The emotive charge which the narrative carried cannot be so transferred owing to its greater inertia and persistence." Accordingly it is "worked off along channels of least resistance in laughter." The real difficulty in transferring, I should think, comes from the matrixes, charges, inertia, channels, and resistance Koestler posits—as though our thoughts were rumbling their way through the Chicago switching yard.[6]

By contrast, René Girard is the contemporary theorist who most lightly reads back from physical laughter to mental laughter. He begins with the idea of weeping at tragedy. The eye behaves as though something had to be expelled, a physical analogy to catharsis. Tears are an integral part of laughter, but much more of the body is involved in expulsion. What kind of threat, then, are both tragedy and comedy trying to get rid of? asks Girard. "An individual is trying to assert upon his environment his own individual rule. We laugh when this pretension is suddenly and spectacularly shattered." Thus we claim our own strength is greater than his. Yet the more we laugh, the weaker we get. Thus there must be a balance. "The threat must be both overwhelming and nil; the danger of being absorbed into the pattern which has already devoured the victim of our laughter must be both immediate and non-existent." By this combination we know that "comedy is intellectual tickling."

It is only a hop from intellectual tickling to the most intriguing of these theories of amusement as imitation of physiological laughter: the one that says we will laugh if a finger is pressed five times a second. Dr. Manfred Clynes has invented the theory of "sentics," according to which each basic emotion, such as joy or anger, has a particular expressive (or "orthoessentic") form expressed in any of a number of "output modalities," including tears, sweat, facial expression or body movement, even finger pressure. One can therefore measure a particular sentic state by finger pressure, and Clynes has done just that, graphing the essential finger wiggles for hate, grief, love, sex, and so on. Naturally individuals vary these forms within the usual bell-shaped curves (rather widely, I'd say), but Clynes claims to have isolated the essential forms. They do not differ systematically for men and women, he says, nor do they vary from one culture to another.

Works of art and other people create emotional effects by imposing essentic forms on us. Thus in Michelangelo's *Pietà* the folds of the shroud and the angle of Mary's head express grief, while "the fold proceeding out and upward from the extended arm (lower center) may be experienced as an aspect of hope."

According to Clynes, essentic forms can be experienced abstractly, without any particular content. Thus we laugh (sometimes) at simply the sound of laughter, from a television laugh track or a guffawing machine in front of a fun house, because (says Clynes) we are getting the essentic form of laughter: a chopping motion of breath or voice at five pulses a second. We even laugh, says Clynes, if our finger is pressed "at the right frequency, phase, and angle." Different angles and wave forms of finger pressing will lead to joyful, malicious, or sardonic laughter. Conversely, different angles and wave forms from laughers in response to the same jokes or cartoons reveal personality. All very neat and put forward with an impressive panoply of graphs and photographs.

What can one say? I just don't believe that I would laugh or feel sexually aroused no matter how many times per second someone pressed my finger, but I freely volunteer to put the appropriate finger to the test.

Laughter as Adaptation

The second group of theorists, those who explain the physiological syndrome we call laughter by a biological or adaptive purpose, is larger. The first and one of the most charming I have been able to find is the Renaissance theorist Madius, a.k.a. Vincenzo Maggi. "An unexpected appearance of something ugly without pain" leads to an "involuntary motion of the rational mind, a consequent pouring out of heat [we would say energy], an enlarging of the heart," therefore "a constriction of the midriff . . . and a shortening of the muscles which lead to the sides of the face." "This motion of the heart . . . is granted men by nature for the relaxation of the mind."

Most of the theorists who explain physical laughter as a present or vestigial adaptation are like Madius: their theories hinge on the idea of relaxation or its absence. Darwin, for example, suggested that laughter is the opposite of distress. Distress manifests itself by short, broken expirations and long breathings in. A physiologist amplifies. Laughter is "swift demobilization," a full and immediate relaxation, which speedily disposes of "energizing secretions" that had been called into the bloodstream—adrenalin, I suppose.[7]

A psychoanalytically oriented physiologist begins with the smile: a preparation to suck. Laughter contrasts with the smile. It is a respiratory disturbance like others that occur when loving behavior (*eros* in the broadest sense) is interrupted and the interruption is then removed. A non-Freudian psychologist, however, notes that laughter sends a fuller stream of blood to the brain. Psychologically, it breaks up consecutive thought, producing euphoria and preventing gloomy thinking. Laughter, then, is "Nature's antidote for the sympathetic tendencies."[8]

These speculations based on human physiology contrast with readings of laughter based on animal analogies. A famous idea is that of Anthony Ludovici, who pointed out that when you have listed the significant aspects of the act of laughing, you have given the symptoms of an animal enraged: teeth bared, head raised, harsh barks. He therefore suggested that laughter has a primeval jungle origin in the "showing of teeth" as an indication of challenge or threat. In this vein (although I am not sure how true or how relevant the observation is) Havelock Ellis says that the most ticklish regions correspond to the spots most vulnerable in a fight.

Elias Canetti gives a different animal analogy: laughter is based on the feeling of pleasure aroused by prey or food that seems certain. We laugh *instead* of eating the individual who has had a pratfall. This idea echoes Hobbes. We laugh instead of eating what we are superior to. One can, apparently, induce laughter in hyenas by putting food before them and taking it away.[9]

Arthur Koestler has also derived laughter from our animal ancestry. It is one of many of our physiological responses that echo threats or promises from the remote past of our species. We jump at a sudden sound. We get gooseflesh when chalk screeches on a blackboard so that our long-lost body hairs will bristle at the attack cry of some extinct beast. We sweat before an examination to dispose of the excessive heat our bodies might develop in the coming fight with the examiner. Those are "overstatements of the body," and so is laughter. The slight malice or lust of a joke serves as a "quasi-homeopathic" stimulus to release adrenalin, which triggers a body reaction, laughter, which is excessive for this slight stimulus, an anachronism.[10]

Other writers on laughter as an adaptation accent its communicative function (as Freud noted how the laughter of the joke hearer absolves the joke teller of guilt). The anthropologist Mary Douglas, for example, contrasts laughter with other bodily interruptions of speech, such as hiccoughs and sneezing. These spasms disrupt the normal parallelism between the body as a channel of communication and our speech, but we screen them out as irrelevant noise. Laughter, however, is always taken to be a communication, although different cultures allot different thresholds to it and different loads of social meaning.

Other suggestions are that laughter serves to show to other humans a willingness to cooperate and a desire to continue with whatever activity is in progress, while crying indicates unwillingness to continue. Laughter was originally a vocal signal to other members of the group that they might relax with safety. Laughter expresses, maintains, and communicates a mood in which the organism feels no need to make any further adjustment to its environment. Laughter is a disguise within which one can communicate secret, forbidden ideas, because it makes people aware of mutual identifications and social relations. It is thus a reflex of disarmament, "a remnant of ancient biological adaptational response in the service of communication, camouflage, mimicry, and the reflex of capitulation."[11]

The ethologist Konrad Lorenz confirms this last idea, "the reflex of capitulation," from observations of animals. Following Kant, he asserts that "most jokes provoke laughter by building up a tension which is then suddenly and unexpectedly exploded. Something very similar may happen in the greeting ceremonies of many animals: dogs, geese, and probably other animals, break into intensive greeting when an unpleasantly tense conflict situation is suddenly relieved." From his point of view, "laughter, like greeting, tends to create a bond." It "diverts aggression" and also produces "a feeling of social unity."

Other writers compare human laughing and smiling to that of apes. Smiling corresponds to the silent bared-teeth display of apes, which represents nonhostility, social attachment, and friendliness, and which overcomes uncertainty about the relationship. Laughter corresponds to the apes' relaxed, open-mouth display, "a metacommunicative signal, designating the behaviours with which it is associated as mock-aggression or play." Darwin observed that apes laugh and chuckle on being tickled. Laughter in humans, then, may be a leftover from our biological heritage. Disruption of breathing actually disadvantages the laugher in a fight, but as a signal it appeases the opponent.[12]

Desmond Morris, the zoologist, points (as René Girard does) to the similarity between crying and laughing: muscular tension, blood to the head, tears, mouth open, lips pulled back, exaggerated breathing, and high-pitched, rasping vocalizations. Laughing evolves from crying. Once the child recognizes its mother as "special" compared to other people, any startling action of hers leads to a mixed stimulus: something frightening from the person who represents security, hence a danger that need not be taken seriously. "The child gives a response that is half a crying reaction and half a parental-recognition gurgle. The magic combination produces a laugh. (Or, rather, it did, way back in evolution. It has since become fixed and fully developed as a separate, distinct response in its own right.)" So the laugh says, "I recognize that a danger is not real." It thus becomes a signal for play, like the play grunt of the chimpanzee. As the ape matures, the signal becomes less useful and dies away, but we, who continually test and explore, go on laughing. Whenever we shock ourselves without getting hurt, we laugh with triumph and relief.

According to Morris, just as laughing is a secondary form of crying, so smiling is a secondary form of laughing. In infancy we used the smile to develop the vital bond of attachment we needed for survival. The infant smiles at faces long before it can distinguish other stimuli and thus evokes smiles in return. The smile in effect substitutes for the fur-clinging behavior of less naked apes. As adults, we signal the people we meet that we are mildly apprehensive, therefore not aggressive, therefore friendly and attracted.[13] Thus Morris arrives at about the same ethological explanation of smiling and laughing as the other analogizers between our primate cousins and ourselves: threat overcome.

An alternative, however, comes from the efforts to teach apes to communicate with humans by signs. They achieve, according to one observer, "simple forms of incongruity humor." They can use the word "funny" at least in the sense of funny-odd. If so, then humor is not a vestige of earlier stages in our development. Rather, it is something we became capable of when we first developed a propositional language system.[14] Who knows, then, what heights the apes may reach if they can be funny and also call it funny? They may even become theorists of the comic.

But is that a consummation to be wished? These theories that attribute laughter to relaxation or communication or even meta-communication, although fortified by the latest in ethological, ethnological, and psychophysiological observation, seem almost as speculative to me as Aristotle's or Madius'.

In 1897 G. Stanley Hall (the psychologist who invited Freud to lecture in America in 1905) and Arthur Allin published the results they obtained by circulating a "syllabus" (questionnaire) about tickling and laughing. Like so many people before and after them, they concluded "that all current theories are utterly inadequate and speculative, and that there are few more promising fields for psychological research." And what research they planned! "To apply all the resources of instantaneous photography to collect laughs and smiles in all their stages." "Secondly, the resources of the phonograph should be applied to the vocal utterances of laughter." More "syllabi," of course, and "fourthly, a very careful collection of thousands of the very

best ancient and modern jests, on cards . . . for ready sort-
ing" (shades of IBM). Matters seem not to have improved very
much since then; now psychologists survey their work and resort hopefully to computer modeling of the process of laughter.[15] Does the laughing computer represent an advance over
the laughing ape? Could they both be laughing at people who
theorize about laughter?

Efforts to explain how complex jokes lead to the physical response we call laughter by reading from mind to body or body
to mind remain as speculative to me as they did to Hall and
Allin. I am convinced, however, by some of the observations
of the geneticists and ethologists. First, the capacity for this
particular coordinated muscular activity must be innate (like
walking or sneezing). Second, this particular muscular cluster
very probably survives as some part of our primate inheritance.

The big problem, however, remains. What is the psychological thread that connects this primitive muscular act (which
in an ape could come from being tickled or in a human from
pseudobulbar palsy) with *Don Quixote* or *Le Misanthrope* or *The
Tempest*? It just does not seem likely to me that the overstuffed
Victorian researches proposed by Hall and Allin will yield that
elfin comic thread. Nor has the even more relentless scientism
of today's streamlined psychologists found it. We need to ask
about the way we are asking, "Why do we laugh?"

But I am getting ahead of myself.

6 Catharsis

If you were to invite to one party all the people who have written about the catharsis we are afforded by comic art, the weight of brains could bend the floorboards. Just for openers, standing there swapping jokes and experiences with jokes would be Plato, Aristotle, Hegel, Marx, Coleridge, and Kierkegaard. Yet despite all those brains (or because of them), their remarks on the subject scatter like the conversation at any old cocktail party. They show nothing like the easy acceptance by centuries of critics of Aristotle's idea of a tragic catharsis.

Aristotle promised us a definition of catharsis, but either he never got round to it or it has been lost in the centuries. Tragedy, he said, dealt "with incidents arousing pity or fear, wherewith to accomplish its catharsis of such emotions." Pity we feel because we stand at a distance from the tragic victim, fear because we identify with him and fear that the same could happen to us (or so I understand him). Aristotle's concept may also have a ritual meaning. He may be saying that we push off our undesirable emotions on the tragic protagonist (like a scapegoat in a ritual) and kill them with him. He may mean that in the situation of drama our passions are raised and allayed in a purer, simplified way, in a "model" situation. Classicists have been debating for centuries just what Aristotle meant, but in a sense it doesn't matter, because he gave us a word with which to settle our thinking: catharsis. Whatever it is, tragedy does it. So, at least, most theorists of literature agree.[1]

Perhaps, however, the notion of catharsis does not really apply to comedy, for so many writers, starting with Aristotle, have regarded the comic as distinctly inferior to tragedy. "Poetry," he said, "diverged in two directions, according to the individual character of the writers. The graver spirits imitated noble actions, and the actions of good men. The more trivial sort imitated the actions of meaner persons." Both tragedy and comedy deal with human limitations, then, but tragedy presents them as large and star-crossed, part of the ultimate structure of life. Comedy presents them as something more trivial and local.

All this the Preacher said long ago, and most eloquently (Eccles. 7:2–4): "It is better to go to the house of mourning, than to go to the house of feasting: for that is the end of all men; and the living will lay it to his heart. Sorrow is better than laughter: for by the sadness of the countenance the heart is made better. The heart of the wise is in the house of mourning; but the heart of fools is in the house of mirth." Perhaps, then, the comic is so earthbound that we cannot say it leads to catharsis in Aristotle's large sense.

How *might* his concept of catharsis apply to comedy, though? Aristotle's treatise on comedy is lost to us, but a diligent classicist, Lane Cooper, has drawn on the tenth-century quasi-Aristotelian *Tractatus Coislinianus* to build an Aristotelian theory of comedy to fill the gap. In it comedy has a catharsis analogous to tragedy's. Anger substitutes for pity and envy for fear. Anger we feel through our distance from the comic victim: we resent his foolishness. Envy we feel because we identify with him and hope his happy ending will happen to us (or so I read Cooper).

To some extent, modern psychologists confirm this idea of catharsis. Hostile humor reduces the aggressive responses of audiences, but nonhostile humor seems to do so too, and some researchers report no reduction. A sociologist suggests that in drama irony in particular helps this cathartic process. When the audience knows something the characters don't know, they feel safe. Hence they can identify with the characters' fear, embarrassment, and anger for the catharsis of those feelings.[2]

A simpler concept of comic catharsis has been in existence for a long time, the idea that comedy acts out a revolt against control. The Earl of Shaftesbury gave it an early-eighteenth-century phrasing: "The natural free spirits of ingenious men, if imprisoned and controlled, will find out other ways of motion to relieve themselves in their constraint: and whether it be in burlesque, mimicry, or buffoonery, they will be glad at any rate to vent themselves." More recently, we would speak of escaping "conformity" or transcending our "inferiorities."[3]

At the end of the nineteenth century, the psychologists Hall and Allin announced scientific support for the idea that the comic frees. "No doubt, like occasional crying for babies, it [laughter] is good for the voice, lungs, diaphragm and digestion, produces needed increase of blood pressure to irrigate new forming tissues, develops arterial tonicity and elasticity . . ." and so on, as though comedy were the snake oil in the medicine show of life.

Oddly, despite this widespread belief that comedy vents our rebellious spirits, much the most common idea about comic catharsis is that comedy teaches us the worldly wisdom of acceptance. At its best, such writers say, the comic makes people urbane, civilized, refined—thus George Meredith in the most famous English essay on comedy: "The test of true comedy is that it shall awaken thoughtful laughter." Comedy, he concludes, corrects vanity, egoism, and sentimentality, restoring us to the belief that "our state of society is founded in common sense," hence to the amused perception of the ways we fall short of that ideal. I find it pleasingly progressive that this Victorian man should conclude that in ages when the Comic Spirit has flourished, civilization has treated women as the equals of men.

Earlier, in Enlightenment Germany, the great theorist of drama Gotthold Lessing wrote that the comic is a "preservative." It allows "the practice of our powers to discover the ridiculous, to discover it easily and quickly under all cloaks of passion and fashion, in all admixtures of good and bad qualities, even in the wrinkles of solemn earnestness." "The instruction of Comedy," according to his Romantic compatriot Schlegel, is "the doctrine of prudence; the morality of consequences and not of motives. Morality, in its genuine acceptation, is essentially allied to the spirit of Tragedy. . . . Comedy is intended . . . to make us shrewder; and this is its true and only possible morality."

Such modern critics as Kenneth Burke and Northrop Frye reach the same conclusion. "Comedy deals with *man in society*, tragedy with *cosmic man*," says Burke. And for Frye, comedy's "significance . . . is ultimately social significance, the establishing of a desirable society." You could say that comedy deals with the golden mean or, alternatively, that a witticism stretches the values of a group in order to get someone to laugh. The laughter, however, is a sign that the laugher has reasserted those values and hence the solidity of the group to which they belong. Hence there is a limit on purely psychological theories of laughter: the laugher may laugh not for wholly intrapsychic reasons, but in response to the purposes of the joke *teller*. You could put it this way: humor has to do with cognitive development, laughter with social development.[4]

This view of the comic leads to a merely instrumental idea of its moral function. Thus the fourth-century grammarian Donatus says, "Comedy is a story of various habits and customs of public and private affairs, from which one may learn what is of use in life and what must be avoided." The comic becomes simply a social corrective. Therefore it requires poetic justice, as the Renaissance English poet George Whetstone said, "for by the rewarde of the good the good are encouraged in wel doinge: and with the scowrge of the lewde the lewde are feared from euill attempts."

The playwrights of the English Restoration, beleaguered by Puritan critics, the Moral Majority of the late seventeenth century, took this way of justifying their wit. John Dryden insisted that comedy does not so much punish faults as make them ridiculous; it deals with forgivable frailties rather than obnoxious crimes—but this, too, is a legitimate moral purpose. William Congreve defined true comedy as the presentation of characters with "humours" both diverting and excessive, a "humour" being a "singular and unavoidable manner of doing, or saying anything, Peculiar and Natural to one Man only; by which his Speech and Actions are distinguish'd from those of other Men."

One could generalize this point of view by saying that the subject matter of comedy is "the abnormal" set against a social norm. Thus, for example, a modern semioticist, who takes the cause of laughter to be the collision of natural law with cultural universes of discourse, thinks the comic catharsis purely the keeping of social balance. Laughter "warns man automatically . . . when he stretches beyond the safety limit in the direction of either culture or nature."[5]

Social theories of the comic tend to limit it to one of its subspecies, satire. W. H. Auden stated the two commonest satirical devices: presenting the human object of the satire as if he were mad and unaware of what he is doing, or presenting him as if he were wicked and completely conscious of what he is doing, without any feeling of guilt. This second category takes in such palpable rogues as Chaucer's Pardoner, Ben Jonson's Volpone, and Shakespeare's Falstaff and Autolycus, while the first, broader method includes the fools, gulls, and zanies who are the stock victims of comedy.

From an ethological point of view, Konrad Lorenz sees in this type of corrective laughter one of the best hopes for controlling our deadly intraspecies aggression, the enthusiastic wars of nation against nation in the service of some ideal that could destroy us all. Laughter can substitute for an attack, because it both creates a bond among those who laugh at the same thing and draws a line against outsiders who either do not laugh or are laughed at. But laughter, Lorenz says, unlike enthusiasm, is always controlled by reason. Hence laughter is the best of lie detectors. It punctures the pomposity or arrogance of those Tartuffes and Hitlers who would have us cheat ourselves by stirring up our dangerously aggressive enthusiasm with false ideals. "Humor exerts an influence on the social behavior of man which, in one respect, is strictly analogous to that of moral responsibility: it tends to make the world a more honest and, therewith, a better place." The twentieth-century scientist Lorenz was echoing the eighteenth-century philosopher Francis Hutcheson: "Nothing is so properly applied to the *false Grandeur*, either of Good or Evil, as Ridicule: Nothing will sooner prevent our excessive Admiration."

In sum, one major group of theorists says comedy restores us to social norms. Another major group says just the opposite. Laughter and the comic can have a revolutionary force and do just exactly what Lorenz thought they would not do—stir up our aggressive enthusiasm. Thus Bernard Shaw put teeth in Meredith's bland formulations: "The function of comedy . . . is nothing less than the destruction of old-fashioned morals." Shaw could have been following his mentor, Karl Marx, who had said, "The final phase of a world-historical form is its comedy. The Greek gods, already once mortally wounded, tragically, in Aeschylus' *Prometheus Bound*, had to die once more, comically, in the dialogues of Lucian. Why does history proceed in this way? So that mankind will separate itself happily from its past." The comic as defense against loss—Marx's idea sounds almost Freudian.

Anthropologists have found that some cultures use this revolution or destruction precisely to conserve the social structure. Primitive societies develop "joking relationships." One person is permitted or even required to tease and make fun of another, using speech or gestures that would be outrageous in another context, and the other is not to take offense. In our society, the Washington press corps periodically "roasts" the president, and in this special joking relationship, the reporters are expected to be irreverent and the president to be amused.

Among anthropologists, however, there is some disagree-

ment as to whether one can attribute to such joking relationships the same function in all societies or whether one has to
examine the interactions within one particular society. Structural anthropologists such as A. R. Radcliffe-Brown compare
joking relations in many societies and arrive at a single function. These joking relations are ways of dealing with situations
(often created by marriage in cultures less political than that of
Washington) in which taboos separate individuals (such as in-
laws) so as to make their interests diverge. They could easily
become enemies, but the society can require them to have a
joking relationship that keeps them together without conflict.[6]

Relying on Freud, the like-minded Mary Douglas interprets
the social addition made by jokes this way: "A dominant pattern of relations is challenged by another." "A joke is a play
upon form . . . [in which] one accepted [social] pattern is challenged by the appearance of another which in some way was
hidden in the first." Hence the joke gives "an exhilarating
sense of freedom from form in general." In this sense, "a joke
is by nature an anti-rite," and "the joker should be classed as a
kind of minor mystic . . . one of those people who pass beyond
the bounds of reason and society and give glimpses of a truth
which escapes through the mesh of structured concepts," a
"ritual purifier." Thus the joke, although it may have no formal
philosophical interpretation in its own culture, may nevertheless "be concerned with problems about the relation of thought
to experience which are . . . a universal pre-occupation of philosophy." The joke provides "an image of the conditions of
human knowledge." For example, many of the parables in the
New Testament are jokes, she says, but we cannot see them in
this light because we do not know the social structure that
would define them as joking: the owner of a vineyard who
pays his workers the same whether they start work at morning, noon, or evening, perhaps; the unjust steward who con-
nived with his master's debtors; or the father who rewards the
prodigal more than the hard-working son. Douglas thus shows
that confining the comic catharsis to purely social matters can

nevertheless lead to the other major idea of comic catharsis, religion.[7]

One can expand the idea of comedy as social in still a third direction, not toward correction or revolution but toward what Harold H. Watts has called "the sense of regain": "a repossession of objects that some part of our being should say farewell to without a sigh." Editor Norman Cousins had old Marx Brothers movies run in his hospital room so that his laughter would help him fight off cancer. In this vein, the medieval philosopher John Tzetzes called comedy "constructive of life," and this is also the feeling the modern philosopher Susanne Langer gives it: "Because comedy abstracts, and reincarnates for our perception, the motion and rhythm of living, it enhances our vital feeling, much as the representation of space in painting enhances our awareness of visual space. The virtual life on the stage is not diffuse and only half felt, as actual life usually is: . . . [but] intensified, speeded up, exaggerated . . ." "This human life feeling is . . . at once religious and ribald, knowing and defiant, social and freakishly individual."

If we read the comic as affirming life, we arrive at a catharsis through enlargement. Comedy becomes "the rest of the bitter truth, a holy impropriety," says the drama critic Walter Kerr. It blurts "out the one thing that was on the tip of everyone's tongue but that everyone was refraining from mentioning." We enlarge our ideas. We achieve a moment of logical truth as we find some underlying cancellation.[8]

The religious critic Nathan Scott, for example, reads the comic catharsis as Christian in a more modern sense. It involves "a restoration of our confidence in . . . the daily occasions of our earth-bound career as being not irrelevant inconveniences but as possible roads into what is ultimately significant in life." A comic hero such as Falstaff gives us "joy . . . in the discovery of how stout and gamy the human thing really is." "The Christian imagination does not shrink . . . from the tangibility, from the gross concreteness, of our life in time, and . . . the limited, conditional nature of human existence." "It believes that God's way of dealing with us is by and through the things and creatures of this world . . ." "It believes that in the Incarnation God Himself has affirmed the world . . . the realm of finitude, the realm of nature and of history." The tragic man finds in his human stuff and his conditional life "a profound embarrassment and perhaps even a curse." The comic man admits he is only human, knowing that that admission "is itself the condition of his life being tolerable."

From another, similar Christian point of view, jokes try to close the gap between the finite and the infinite, and "the comedy lies in the protagonist's final realization of the disappearance of the chasm between the two." The truly serious man "realizes that the grossly human and the grandly sublime within himself are wonderfully and repugnantly mixed." Thus "the structure of dramatic comedy and the structure of Christ's passionate action bear an analogical relation to each other," Christ being, like the comic protagonist, a victor because he is a victim.[9]

In short, the comic lends itself to a specifically Christian reading if one interprets its emphasis on the low and earthy as an affirmation of what a Christian God has given humans. Another notion of the comic, however, has it doing just the opposite of regaining or affirming everyday life: the comic involves a certain detachment from the things we laugh at, what the philosopher Henri Bergson called a "momentary anaesthesia of the heart" and the poet Richard Eberhart "an intellectual disrespect to the deepest urges of man."

Comedy, then, involves a duality, a mixture of acceptance and rejection, or, as Plato said in the *Philebus*, of pleasure and pain. "When we laugh at the folly of our friends, pleasure, in mingling with envy, mingles with pain. . . . And the argument implies that there are combinations of pleasure and pain in lamentations, and in tragedy and comedy, not only on the stage, but on the greater stage of human life." "In the comedy that we call life," says Cervantes' Don Quixote, "some play the part of emperors, others that of pontiffs—in short, all the characters that a drama may have—but when it is all over, that is to say, when life is done, death takes from each the garb that differentiates him, and all at last are equal in the grave." Thus, even if it ends with death, life is comic, if only we can keep our cool. "I commended mirth," said the Preacher, in another mood (Eccles. 8:15), "because a man hath no better thing under the sun, than to eat, and to drink, and to be merry: for that shall abide with him."

Perhaps, then, the comic catharsis is simply the creation of a cynical detachment—the ability to feel that "all the world's a stage." Perhaps we can go further. The literary theorist Wylie Sypher notes, "From the anthropologist's point of view the tragic action, however inspiring and however perfect in artistic form, runs through only one arc of the full cycle of drama; for the entire ceremonial cycle is birth: struggle: death: resurrection. The tragic arc is only birth: struggle: death. Consequently the range of comedy is wider than the tragic range—perhaps more fearless—and comic action can risk a different sort of purgation and triumph."

This larger range the great comic writers have known from the first. Aristophanes in *The Frogs* sets his artistic consideration of tragedy within the comic framework of death and rebirth. So also Chaucer, bidding farewell to his *Troilus and Criseyde* ("litel myn tragedye"), prays for strength "to make in som comedye," then sends his dead hero up to heaven, where he laughs at the woe of those who weep for his death and pleads with lovers to love God and remember that all this world is but a country fair that fades as fast as flowers. Both writers set the single tragic episode, as so many of Shakespeare's tragedies do, within a larger cyclic, and so more hopeful, conception of reality.

The tragic emphasizes the uniqueness and finality of human experience, claims Maynard Mack, while the comic emphasizes permanence and typicality. The comic makes us see the things that are terribly unique and final to us in the larger perspective of the whole of human life, or, indeed, from the perspective

of God. "Comedy, then," writes James Feibleman, the aes-
thetician, "criticizes the finite for not being infinite,"[10] and we
can ask, with Epictetus, "What else is tragedy but the perturba-
tions of men who value the externals exhibited in that kind of
poetry?"

The comic catharsis thus enables us to achieve a duality of
acceptance and rejection, or as Robert Graves says, "a faculty
of seeing apparently incongruous elements as part of a scheme
for supra-logical necessity." To the same end, Baudelaire could
argue that, since laughter "is essentially human, it is also essentially contradictory, that is to say, it is at once a sign of
infinite grandeur and infinite wretchedness: of infinite wretchedness by comparison with the absolute Being who exists as an
idea in Man's mind; of an infinite grandeur by comparison
with the animals." Hence, every effort to represent God must
become ridiculous, but at the same time (from this Augustinian
point of view) representations of humans become ridiculous
because without God humans can do nothing.[11]

Out of this duality of acceptance and abasement, says Ernst
Cassirer, we execute a movement of transcendence. "Comic art
. . . can accept human life with all its defects and foibles, its
follies and vices. . . . We see this world in all its narrowness, its
pettiness, and silliness. We live in this restricted world, but we
are no longer impressed by it. Such is the peculiar character
of the comic catharsis. Things and events begin to lose their
material weight; scorn is dissolved into laughter and laughter is
liberation."

Tragedy, in this view, pins us down to the contradictions of
reality; comedy allows us to transcend them. Thus Hegel saw
in the comic the triumphant self-assertion of the purely personal soul-life over all other forms of experience. He therefore
made comedy the "very consummation" of the dialectic process in art. Nietzsche, too, could speak of the comic "as the
artistic release from the nausea of the absurd."

So also Plato in the good but not perfect republic of the *Laws*
found a place for comic poets (subject to regulation), for "it is

necessary also to consider and know uncomely persons and thoughts, and those intended to produce laughter . . . for serious things cannot be understood without laughable things, nor opposites at all without opposites, if a man is really to have intelligence of either; but he cannot carry out both in action, if he is to have any degree of virtue." Tragic poets, however, he rejects from society, "for our whole state is an imitation of the best and noblest life which we affirm to be indeed the very truth of tragedy." In the ideal republic of the *Republic*, the world of pure action, Socrates argues that "even when two species of imitation are nearly allied, the same persons cannot succeed in both, as, for example, the writers of tragedy and comedy," and he banishes all literature as an imitation pandering to pleasure rather than truth. At the end of the *Symposium*, however, after Socrates had given his companions a glimpse of the Highest, "there remained only Socrates, Aristophanes [representing comedy], and Agathon [representing tragedy] who were drinking out of a large goblet which they passed round, and Socrates was discoursing to them, . . . compelling the other two to acknowledge that the genius of comedy was the same with that of tragedy, and that the true artist in tragedy was an artist in comedy also. To this they were constrained to assent, being drowsy, and not quite following the argument. And first of all, Aristophanes dropped off, then, when the day was already dawning, Agathon."

This Platonic mingling of discourse and drama, as I read it, proves that comedy and tragedy are alike because they are, like the dialogue itself, minglings. Action demands tragic seriousness, while contemplation demands comic wisdom. In this realistic world, the world of the *Laws* and the *Symposium* as opposed to the ideal world of the *Republic*, action and contemplation mingle, as do pleasure and pain. Hence tragedy and comedy are at bottom much the same, since both represent these mixtures. Moreover, in this world, contemplation has to come before action. Hence comedy, which provides a frame of reference, is more necessary to society than tragedy, which shows only the best and noblest (although tragedy is therefore closer to the dawn of philosophical wisdom).

I think realist philosophers (starting with Aristotle) have tended to prefer tragedy, while idealist philosophers (starting with Plato) have preferred comedy. If so, it should be no surprise that the most exalted and delicate idea of the comic catharsis was produced by Kierkegaard. Kierkegaard regarded himself as being in the Socratic tradition of the philosophic *eiron*, "talking like a madman." For him "the mode of apprehension of the truth is precisely the truth." He is therefore difficult, indeed impossible, to summarize.

For Kierkegaard, "what lies at the root of both the comic and the tragic . . . is the discrepancy, the contradiction between the infinite and the finite, the eternal and that which becomes." The tragic leaves the individual pinned to this discrepancy and therefore suffering. The comic rises above it to painlessness. Through irony an individual can rise above the "aesthetic" life of immediate sensation to the intense self-awareness of the "ethical" man. Beyond the ethical life, the religious man, totally aware of his own inward self and through it totally aware of the absolute, infinite Idea, insulates himself from all activity (while not becoming inactive) by humor. It "is always a . . . recollecting what is behind, manhood's recollection of childhood . . . the backward perspective." "When viewed from a direction looking toward the Idea, the apprehension of the discrepancy between the infinite and finite is pathos; when viewed with the Idea behind one, the apprehension is comic." Thus one's comic sensibility marks the extent to which one has transcended ordinary concerns (sensation, ethical conduct) and moved toward the Absolute.[12] (So that Plato should have shown Aristophanes lasting into the dawn, not Agathon.)

Kierkegaard is a Western mystic, but Eastern mysticism leads William I. Thompson to the same trancendence. All comic forms tend toward the twentieth century's "comedy of the absurd," which rests on our knowledge that "human beings who pretend to a knowledge of truth are preposterously funny." Such is the laughter of Krishna, "a supra-human (or inhuman, if you will) point of view."

The comic catharsis, then, is (from these various Platonic or quasi-Platonic viewpoints) a resolution through transcendence of one, some, or many of the incongruities of this world (our attempts at knowledge, government, virtue, love, or riches). The Platonic comic is an unmasking, yes, but the effect of this unmasking is to take the comic butt out of the cycles of folly, affectation, and imperfection and to put the merely human into a relation of possibility toward the more-than-human.[13]

"The happy ending of the fairy tale, the myth, and the divine comedy of the soul is to be read, not as a contradiction, but as a transcendence of the universal tragedy of man," says the mythologist Joseph Campbell. "The objective world remains what it was, but, because of a shift of emphasis within the subject, is beheld as though transformed. Where formerly life and death contended, now enduring being is made manifest— as indifferent to the accidents of time as water boiling in a pot is to the destiny of the bubble, or as the cosmos to the appearance and disappearance of a galaxy of stars. Tragedy is the shattering of the forms and of our attachment to the forms; comedy, the wild and careless, inexhaustible joy of life invincible."

"In humor," said Coleridge, more simply, "the little is made great and the great little, in order to destroy both, because all is equal in contrast with the infinite." I might add, as a final comic note, that Coleridge lifted this uplifting idea from Jean Paul Richter.

But what can *we* lift from this rather astonishing diversity? We can reduce all these various views to an outline:

1. Social correction
   a. Restoration to desired conduct
   b. Social revolution
   c. Affirmation of life within society

2. Religious catharsis
   a. Affirming life as God's gift
   b. Rejection of life as low and sinful
3. Transcendence
   a. Both acceptance and rejection of
      i. life as low
      ii. the effort to reach beyond life
   b. A mysticism that transcends both acceptance and rejection

When set out that way, the ideas seem to me wildly inconsistent. Some theorists say the comic reconciles us to society, others that it makes us revolt against society. Some say the comic commits us to life, others that it commits us to reject life. Some say the comic has only social meaning, others that it enables us to transcend the merely social, indeed takes us to mystical levels that go beyond religion itself.

Despite these contradictions, however, I can glean a nugget of agreement. For one thing, the comic catharsis has to do either with society (or earthy or bodily life) or with religious ideas of a plane beyond this world. Further, I think that, by and large, all the various authors set the comic catharsis in the context of certain contrasts. One has to do with acceptance and rejection, the other with transcendence as against being pinned down to something. And the something? That ranges from earthiness to the human body to a particular set of social circumstances to a religious stance to some point of view that transcends even religion.

These various ideas of the comic catharsis hover between acceptance and rejection; between being caught in something as opposed to transcending it; between the earthy or worldly or social and whatever is beyond our experience of this world. In other words, we could say the comic catharsis is either transcendence of or submission to or the acceptance or rejection of society, the body, earthly life, religion, or transcendence itself. Surely that covers just about everybody at our hypothetical gathering of writers on the comic catharsis.

What is striking to me, however, is that all these ideas of the comic catharsis have a shifting, shimmering quality. They don't stay put. One doesn't just learn something from *Don Quixote*, put it in a mental pocket, and carry it away. Rather, the comic catharsis (unlike, I would say, the tragic) remains a moving, dialectical thing: one actively submits to or transcends or accepts or rejects—and one does more than one of those things at once.

I notice something else, too, about this collection of theories. They all derive from, at most, introspection. Unlike the psychologists, none of these writers brings forward any outside evidence. None of them suggests any reason for saying, "This theory is right and that one is wrong," except perhaps for one's own feeling that this or that theory rings true to one's own experience. Yet none of these writers has made any effort to set down that experience, either his own or anyone else's. That says something to me about a road not taken in this march through the comic.

II HOW CAN WE ASK?

7 Theorists Theorizing

As this thicket of theorists demonstrates, we humans have devoted a quite extraordinary amount of talent and genius to the question "Why do people laugh?" We have been asking that question for more than two thousand years. And the result?

We could organize these theories of laughter, the comic, or humor into an outline like that in Table 1. We could even compress the outline into a single sentence:

If we perceive a sudden, playful incongruity that gratifies conscious and unconscious wishes and defeats conscious and unconscious fears to give a feeling of liberation, then we laugh.

We laugh—or we don't.

Perhaps, like Queen Victoria, we are not amused. Or we feel just a little bit like laughing. That is the problem with such an if–then formula: the stimulus may be as laughable as all get-out, the conditions may be just right, the joke may meet one of the comic patterns, and a busful of bishops may have told us that the joke achieves religious transcendence—but we still don't laugh. Or perhaps, as Bella Abzug complained of some political shenanigan, "It makes you laugh, but it's not funny."

Another problem is that a one-sentence if–then does not describe the timing of even the crudest stand-up comic. It says next to nothing about the form of the simplest joke. It certainly cannot tell me anything about the marvels of detailed self-torment that Molière's Alceste achieves. It cannot tell me why a

TABLE 1. Theories of humor: Why do people laugh?

I. Stimulus: incongruity
   a. Cognitive: simultaneous affirmation and negation
   b. Ethical: between things as they are and as they ought to be
   c. Formal: between content and form
II. Conditions
   a. Playfulness
   b. Suddenness
III. Psychology
   a. Archetype theories
   b. Psychologies of consciousness
     i. Relief theories
     ii. Superiority theories
   c. Psychoanalytic theories
   d. Experiments
IV. Physiology
   a. Laughter as innate action cluster
   b. Laughter as physical reflection of mental movements
   c. Laughter as adaptive communication
V. Catharsis
   a. Social correction
     i. Restoration to desired conduct
     ii. Social revolution
     iii. Affirmation of life over society
   b. Religious catharsis
     i. Affirmation of life as God's gift
     ii. Rejection of life as low
   c. Transcendence
     i. Both acceptance and rejection of both low life and beyond-life
     ii. A mysticism transcending all

Thurber cartoon traced by someone else (as in the psychologists' tests) loses its charm. It gives no clue as to why, as Mark Twain said, "the difference between the right word and the almost right word is like the difference between lightning and the lightning-bug."

As Table 1 suggests, the point in the comic transaction where theorists have been most various is the end: the sense of catharsis. How can one render that elusive, mystical mingling of acceptance, rejection, transcendence, and compromise which even a modest one-liner makes possible, to say nothing of a comic masterpiece such as *The Frogs* or *The Sea Gull*?

When one has been asking a question for a long, long time and a great deal of thought and effort have yielded only a sort of half-success, it seems to me worth considering the possibility that the question can be posed more successfully another way. It may have been cast in such terms that no answer is possible.

Most theorists of the comic have been asking, "At what do we laugh?"; "Under what conditions do we laugh?"; and, most insistently, "Why do we laugh?" Behind all such questions is the assumption that they have an answer, that is, that there is some isolable reason that *we*, people in general, laugh, and that the important thing is to find it.

Certainly the idea has plausibility. I can tickle just about anybody and get a laugh. I can give just about anybody nitrous oxide and get a laugh. I can tell a joke and most of an audience will laugh. The notion that there are stimuli, conditions, psychological principles, physiological dynamisms, or moral aims that lead people in general, a "we," to laugh seems a reasonable assumption from which to proceed. On the other hand, suppose we were to ask, "Why do people cry?" Would we not get the same sort of hodgepodge we have gotten for laughter, these twenty-four centuries of inquiry leading to no conclusive explanation?

One problem, I think, is that a psychological question about mental dynamics has gotten mixed with a physiological question about a bodily process. Laughter is a cluster of physiological moves. If it were pathological, we would call the movements a syndrome: the rapid, excessive breathing and expulsion of air, the drawing up of the facial muscles, the contraction of the throat, and so on.

All human beings use essentially the same cluster of movements, whatever their era, color, gender, or culture. Like our ability to fall and recover ourselves some fifty or a hundred times a minute and so walk upright on two feet, this complex combination of nervous and muscular activity we call laughter must be inherited, as our physiologist of laughter suggests. As with walking, sneezing, binocular vision, weeping, and a host of other human abilities (perhaps including language), it would be satisfying to know the genetic basis for such general-within-the-species clusters of nervous and mental actions. It would also be satisfying to know how physiological stimuli put that system into action. Nitrous oxide, tickling, and certain forms of epilepsy do start people laughing, and it would greatly interest me, anyway, to know why.

For the time being, however, the physical act of laughing remains a mysteriously separate, intact, almost self-contained physiological process. Some physical or mental event sets it off. Then its effects—the chest and belly convulsions, the hyperventilation, that toothy feeling about the mouth, the stiffness in the throat—these effects feed back into our perception of the original event. Our body tells us—proves, really—that the event was funny. In trying to explain laughter, we can talk about that event (as in the stimulus and the psychological theories); we can talk about the sensations our laughing body sends back to our amused minds; but the physiological laugh itself remains a special system with its own rules.

If laughing is inherited, it probably serves some primate function. Perhaps someday we shall learn it from observations of our fellow primates. Even if we do, though, I doubt if we shall be able to read back from that primitive hominid function to the dynamics of civilized laughter at *Tristram Shandy* or even *Lolita*.

The problem (again) is that we laugh at too great a range of things—from nitrous oxide to *Nicholas Nickleby*. The function that laughter may once have served for our hominid ancestors has been overshadowed by the complex, puzzling set of stimuli, conditions, and psychological processes described in Chapters 2, 3, and 4. We can hope that with the current interest in inherited abilities, the next decades will see greater understanding of laughter along with other psychosomatic clusters. Molecular biologists, brain physiologists, geneticists, and many polymaths have shown remarkable progress in the last two decades in discovering gene patterns and clusters and their functions. No doubt they will be able before long to tell us something about how we inherit the ability to laugh. Meanwhile, however, we shall be more successful, I think, if we postpone trying to "read" this physiological cluster and simply accept it as such.

That is, we can consider the physical act of laughing a self-regulating system (like walking or perceiving distances) in the service of higher mental processes. In laughing, some autonomous system within our bodies does the bidding of subtler conscious and unconscious mental processes and in turn feeds back sensations to them. We can explore that feedback loop—that dialogue between self and joke—even though one of its components, physical laughter, is sealed in mystery, provided we can tell what goes into a laugh and what comes out. That we can, more or less, do. What goes in are stimulus, conditions, and psychological gratification—as described in our first three kinds of theories. What comes out is catharsis—the fifth and last kind.

The theories begin to show severe limitations, however, not only when they are rolled up into one big formula, but when they are considered separately. The theory that we laugh at the incongruity between the way things are and the way they ought to be, for example, will not account for someone's failure to laugh at that incongruity. In general, stimulus theories account only for jokes that work; they do not tell us why a joke works for some people but not for others.

Only one of the incongruity or stimulus theories, the Aristotelian incongruity between the harmful and its harmless presentation, addresses the question of comic form, and then only in the most general terms. Yet, as Freud's elaborate study of joke techniques shows, form is of the essence. A slight change in language or timing (just as in a lyric) completely alters the laughability of a joke.

In general, the stimulus theories do not touch the subtleties of either jokes or more complex comic works. One plugs either a simple joke or a work as rich as *The Tempest* into such a formula as Bergson's "the mechanical encrusted upon the living." One locates in *The Tempest* the mechanical (the monotonously villainous villains, perhaps); one locates the living (the lovers, the island); one notes that the one is encrusted upon the other (in Prospero's "art," for example). But so what? Kant's theory or Hazlitt's or Aristotle's will serve equally well. And we still have not dealt with the subtle or elusive details of the comedy.

Moreover, all the different stimulus theories seem to fit, leaving me no reason to prefer one stimulus theory over another. To me, this equivalence poses one of the strangest enigmas of comic theory.

Condition theories make more modest claims. Unlike the stimulus theories, they purport to state only necessary, not sufficient, conditions (no pun intended). We laugh only if the stimulus is sudden or only if the situation (or the "frame" or the metacommunication) is playful, and maybe not then. Condition theories thus provide ways of explaining why someone didn't laugh, and perhaps for that reason, perhaps because of the very modesty of their claims, they do seem more solidly true than the other kinds of theories.

The psychological theories promise more than the others, yet they present many more problems. Archetype, myth-and-ritual theories are basically stimulus theories in psychological clothing: if you show people the appropriate stimulus—a scapegoat ritual, a death-and-rebirth legend, a marriage—they will find it funny and (perhaps) laugh. Archetypal theories thus share the difficulties of other stimulus theories: they do not account for form, for detail, or for the person who doesn't laugh.

More truly psychological are the theories based in psychoanalytic, experimental, or consciousness psychology, for they begin with the laugher rather than what is laughed at. Each points to a different experience. The psychologies of consciousness derive laughter from feelings of hostility or superiority or relief. Psychoanalysis finds an economy—in inhibition (wit), in conscious effort (the comic), or in emotion (humor). To state it the other way round, the laugher laughs from a sudden sense of surplus energy, either as drive (aggressive or sexual) or in the service of ego or superego. The experimentalists locate laughter in a sudden matching of some trait in the laugher with some theme in the joke.

These psychological theories seem more sophisticated to me than theories either about the stimulus to or the conditions for laughter—but they present their own, more sophisticated problems, too. For one thing, they all rely on categories, as the stimulus theories do: one can simply plug different terms into a formula. Yet categories rest on definitions. Some categories sort out types of the laughable into wit, the comic, or humor (as in Freud's comprehensive essay). Some classify drives or fantasies, such as oral, phallic, and oedipal. Others, such as repression, denial, sublimation, and overcompensation, name the defenses one meets in different people. Others simply name "hostility" or "superiority." All such categories, however, present problems of definition so severe that I prefer simply to mention them and run. They ask me to divide continuous psychological transactions into discrete bits and put them in pigeonholes. I find it virtually impossible to say in any nonarbitrary way where one category ends and the next begins.

Categories also present problems of choice. I favor psychoanalytic categories, but someone else has a perfect right to ask whether another set of categories—behaviorist, perhaps, or Jungian—might not fit the seamless web of amusement better, or at least more satisfyingly. Seemingly "objective" categories therefore present interpersonal problems. When did the psychoanalyst ever persuade the behaviorist that his categories were more explanatory? Or vice versa? Reason seems not to prevail in these disputes (or in many others). Similarly, what some psychoanalytic critics mean by "defense" may be very different from what I intend: any strategy a person uses to meet and mesh the world's demands or his body's. Even if we agreed on such a definition, we could never be sure that we meant the same thing by "strategy" or "demand" or "world" or "body." Again, the application even of shared, "scientific" principles rests on interpersonal relationships.

These principles involve another problem—here it comes in the guise of psychic determinism. The stimulus theorists looked from a supposed cause (incongruity, say) to its supposed effect, laughter. The psychologists look the other way and more sophisticatedly: from a dependent to an independent variable; from a feeling of superiority, say, to the sudden gratification of an exhibitionistic impulse through the joke. Both stimulus theorists and experimentalists, however, presuppose a lawlike link between laughter and something else. Indeed, most psychologists—Freud is the classic example—explicitly posit this kind of psychological determinism as the necessary justification for their work.

As with the stimulus theories, though, variability presents a problem. Some people aren't amused. Why does one person get a sense of superiority from a given joke and someone else not? Usually psychologists resort to statistics to allow for variability: not a hard-boiled, one-to-one, cause-and-effect relation, but a softer correlation. Four out of ten people don't laugh at twins, but six out of ten do. Then they try (sometimes) to define that correlation and find out how the four differ from the six. Again, though, that relationship will be expressed not in a hard-and-fast way, but as a correlation of probabilities and likelihoods. The assumption of psychological determinism remains, but in a curiously misty and floating way, as if to say, "These events are caused, of course, but we can't quite say how."

Even so, psychological experimenters are particularly keen on the assumption of psychic determinism, the hope that people can be generalized into categories, and the faith that statistics will correlate them. It is a bit awesome to read an experimental psychologist's Faustian aspirations toward scientific rigor. One noted experimentalist, D. E. Berlyne, for example, writes: "The natural sciences, physics and chemistry, can now predict, control, and explain much of their subject matter with virtual certainty. The behavioral sciences, like psychology, are still a long way from this, although they are advancing progressively in this direction."[1] When I attempted to survey experiments on laughter (including Berlyne's), however, I was both disappointed and reassured. I was disappointed in that I did not find any satisfying explanation of laughter, but reassured that I did not find that steady progression toward control. We human beings still laugh in our untidy, capricious ways despite the aspirations of experimental psychologists to predict or control our amusement. We seem to be too variable for their variables.

Nowhere does this human variability become clearer than in the theories of catharsis. Some theorists see the comic as purely social, others as religious, and still others as transcending reality in some total, metaphysical way. Even within these large categories, theorists differ. Some who believe the comic is purely social think of it as restoring and conservative; others as revolutionary; still others as proclaiming a radical individualism. A religious sense of the comic can lead either to acceptance of earthy life or to its rejection. A transcendent view of the comic can lead either to acceptance of the here-and-now or a flight beyond it.

These differences in theory reflect the subtle feelings one has after laughter or the comic. They quite elude categories, principles of cause and effect, and the experimental techniques of even the most relentless psychologist. They seem to be highly personal. Yet even the religious authors dump all our noble aspirations into a categorical "we," presuming that I share their beliefs and values.

We have looked at nearly two hundred theories and variations on theories. Taken all together (as in table 1), they almost seem to form a coherent system. Just about all of them say something sensible about some aspect of a general human sense of humor. Yet none of them seems to apply to all laughers, nor do they explain why one person laughs at a certain joke and another doesn't. Nor do several different theories combine to form one large explanation. We could apologize for the whole package as the curate did for his egg in the old *Punch* cartoon: "Parts of it are excellent!" Yet a theory, like an egg, ought to satisfy throughout. I think it is time to turn from theories and some presumed *we* to real laughers.

8 *Laughers Laughing*

In short, our two hundred theories and variations of theories mostly ask, "Why do we laugh?" They succeed so fragmentarily that I'd like to try asking, "Why does he or she or you or I—somebody in particular—laugh?" For our stimulus, consider the six cartoons by B. Kliban on the following pages.

I should point out what may already be obvious to you. By no means everyone finds these cartoons funny. The *New York Times* reports that Kliban's first book, *Cats* (1975), proved an immense success. By the beginning of 1978, it had sold 450,000 copies.[1] These cartoons, however, from his second book, *Never Eat Anything Bigger than Your Head & Other Drawings*,[2] get a distinctly mixed reception.

A group of my students agreed to record their reactions and let me convey them to you. "Though I find some . . . interesting," Serge commented, "none made me think of anything worth repeating. I still prefer *Peanuts*." Some responders were friendlier than he, but most simply had fun proclaiming their annoyance. "Kliban (Klee-ban)," wrote Sherry, sneering the name, "should be banned. He should be shot at sunrise. It's not that I don't think he's humorous. It's that I think he's unnecessary (to me)." "I find," Suzette wrote, "I am neither turned on nor off by these so-called 'cartoons.' Instead, I feel the same as I did the day the dentist removed an impacted wisdom tooth, numb from the neck up."

I had asked these students to write what, if anything, they

Carl Meets His Match in Ramon

Short on Brains, but a Terrific Dancer

119

Victor Grows More Suspicious Hourly

Chapter XI

LUCILLE WAS SECRETLY THRILLED
WHEN NORMAN SUCKED HER TOASTER.

found funny in Kliban's cartoons, why they thought they had laughed (or hadn't), and what associations they had with the cartoons. Already, of course, that is a sure-fire way to shut off amusement.

Inevitably, too, explanations and associations shaded into one another. Moreover, the explanations and associations with the individual cartoons varied even more than the verdicts of funny or not funny. In just three comments on the fly cartoon, Silas, Sabrina, and Serge developed three wholly different themes.

Silas talked about the appropriateness or invitability of the fly as a dinner guest. Sabrina observed the truism that today's food is tomorrow's fertilizer. Serge found a comparison of food with trash and brought in a feminist idea: the fly as a woman presumed to have no taste.

Frankly, none of these responses had occurred to me, except perhaps for Serge's first point, "Both are to receive what

---

"I'LL HAVE THE GAZPACHO"

SILAS. Here the fly is a dinner guest. Usually the situation is one where the fly is uninvited, but in Kliban's world flies are appropriate companions at mealtime and may even be great conversationalists.

SABRINA. Despite appearances and the fancy accoutrements, the food will still be turned into shit. The fly's presence alludes to this fact. It is against the grain of our habits to sit in a restaurant having a good meal and think that our food will be the shit of tomorrow.

SERGE. I liked this one better. The verbal humor is based . . . on the abrupt transition from . . . choice food to trash (as seen in human terms) but both are to receive what they value.

Also how men treat their wives when out: ordering for them, perhaps even commenting on how women were assumed to have little knowledge of fine foods, implying that the woman has no taste.

"Cynthia Is Mistakenly Crowned King of Norway"

SILAS. The absurdity makes us laugh because Cynthia walking to her car with a bag full of groceries could be anyone we know . . . when suddenly, she is thrust into royalty—royalty that performs its own shopping. I see this as a psychic projection of a woman who wished secretly to be a man, or [is?] at least envious of men, men who achieve high social status as kings and in her daydream Cynthia becomes king, not queen. She is not only king, while performing mundane chores, but has six men following her to do her will.

SABRINA. It seems that the pomp and ceremony are more important than the event's meaning. It doesn't matter who is crowned just as long as the crown is placed on someone's head. All of the people are carrying something—swords, papers, and the crown. Cynthia carries groceries. The groceries are important while all of the other objects are extraneous. We must eat but we can live without swords, papers, and ceremonies.

SERGE. Very funny. How ludicrous pomp and ceremony are. Military/political/church all represented. What weight does authority hold?

SID. Very funny. For all the results we get from our elected or crowned officials, it might as well happen in this fashion: I mean on a street corner, haphazardly like this. Lucille's expression as the Pope places the crown on her head seems to sum it all up: "What are they about, anyway? I'm just trying to get these heavy packages home, and now they place this dumb, heavy crown on my head." Blind Justice, no? But just one question: how did Richard Nixon or Hitler attain power, if not a case of blundering blindness on we the people's part?

SHERRY. The cartoon . . . suggests the desire for women to be recognized in what they recognize to be man's world. Some women are better at achieving male recognition than others. Is it necessary for a woman to be crowned a king to have really been successful? Rewards are sexually defined.

they value." Different foods are delicacies for different people. When I look at this cartoon, I recall the proverb "One man's meat is another man's poison." (Then, is it significant that the man in the cartoon doesn't order meat?)

The crowning of Cynthia drew a variety of associations and explanations. Silas imagined a woman condemned to mundane chores who secretly wished to be a man. Sabrina thought what was funny was making ceremony more important than groceries. Serge thought the cartoon was a spoof of authority. Sid contrasted the randomness of official power with Lucille's (sic) purposeful shopping. Sherry wrote about the crowning as a male recognition of woman's importance. Again, several themes: woman seeking, desiring, needing man's social status; authority as pointlessly ceremonial, as ludicrous, chancy, weightless, blind, or ineffectual.

The themes overlap. They are both shared and not shared. They differ and do not differ. To me, they all seem equally applicable, yet none defines my own reaction. I find the cartoon funny (to the limited extent that I do) by virtue of the contrast between the routine, random quality of shopping for groceries and the serious, purposeful business of coronation.

"Short on Brains, but a Terrific Dancer" led to other divergences. How do you read the caption? Who is the subject of the caption? Does it refer to the man? That was Sabrina's reading. Does it refer to the man plus the nearest woman? Serge read it that way. One of the women? Sophie thought so. Both women? Sherry seemed to say that.

The drawing of Carl and Ramon led to thoughts of competition, but again with much variation in the particulars. Sabrina talked about appearances. Sherry contrasted the open competition that society allows between men with the covert competition between women. Sid moralized about the pettiness of competition seen from another point of view. Serge contrasted hard, brutal Carl with soft, cultured Ramon.

The thoughtful Victor elicited two odd responses. Sabrina contrasted human brains and bearish functions. Suzette, dis-

---

"Short on Brains, but a Terrific Dancer"

Sabrina. When the woman says that the man is a terrific dancer, she alludes to his physical characteristics. She is really saying that he is a good lover. But, since women are not supposed to be so straightforward in our society, she cannot express herself directly.

Serge. My central question here would be, "Who is the caption referring to?" Is that what the two central figures think of each other?

Sophie. Kliban's drawing makes me uncomfortable. . . . I don't like seeing body parts out of proportion, particularly those piggy or pushy noses displaced/displayed upwards. But also . . . the huge (and surely unevenly sized?) breasts of the "terrific dancer" . . . suddenly it is as if nothing is stable. . . .

Sherry. . . . a stereotype view of women suggesting one has either brains or a "body" but not both, assuming a man certainly has both.

---

gusted, treated the hiding as an image of her own reaction, the bears as symbols of her own anger.

The Lucille cartoon, of course, evoked even more physicality. Sabrina singled out the words "sucked" and "toaster," and wondered whether these people were the type to have oral sex. Sherry picked out "secretly." Sid did a complicated (nervous?) analysis of "the reader's" response, claiming the fantasy was so removed from the probable that Norman and Lucille were dehumanized—by the cartoon, not by Sid. Sophie was baffled by the "adult" emotions.

Puns are gotten and not gotten. Secrets are spotted or not. Identifications happen or they don't. Whatever the reasons, whatever the cartoon, responses, associations, and explanations vary widely. How can we ask why *we* laugh, then? Doesn't *one* have to ask why *one* laughs?

In effect, we can fit our seven laughers laughing (and not laughing) onto a grid. We have a series of six cartoons: the fly, Cynthia, "Short on Brains," Carl and Ramon, Victor, and

Lucille. We could list the cartoons from left to right across the top of the grid. We have seven laughers (and nonlaughers): Silas, Sabrina, Serge, Sid, Sherry, Suzette, and Sophie. (I have been following the experimental psychologists' convention of calling their "subjects" Ss.) We could list them down the left side of the matrix. We could then write each person's response to each cartoon in the appropriate one of the forty-two boxes.

"CARL MEETS HIS MATCH IN RAMON"

SABRINA. One man's appearance receives . . . society's approval, while the other's definitely does not.

SHERRY. Kliban deals with men in a kinder fashion than he does with women. . . . Carl is able to compete out in the open with Ramon. Carl is allowed to fail, but also to continue the contest with an opportunity to get better and possibly succeed. Women, on the other hand, are not treated as freely competitive for fear of being unfeminine.

SID. Great humor—give it 100%. . . . The humor occurs once we realize that a competitive situation is being played out here. Looking at these two characters throws light on our own stupidities, which aren't so obvious to us, for we must be kind and realize the relativity of circumstance and that someone advanced [in relation?] to us might look at our petty academic/sibling rivalries in just this light.

SERGE. Why should I find this funny? Carl—hard sound. Ramon—soft sound. Understatement? Culture versus brutality?

"VICTOR GROWS MORE SUSPICIOUS HOURLY"

SABRINA. This cartoon seems to allude to man's animalistic nature. We are animals with sophisticated brains. Both bears and people shit, only we usually do not do it in the forest.

SUZETTE. . . . a group of people dressed in costumes. To me, they are all candidates for *Soap*. Without a doubt they would probably get the parts too. The only way I can possibly relate to this picture is to hide like Victor until all these cartoons go away, or utilize my animal instincts and tear them apart.

"Lucille Was Secretly Thrilled . . ."

Sabrina. This is obviously sexual. It alludes to oral sex in particular. This couple does not look like the type of people who would have oral sex, but, even though the woman doesn't do it or have it done, she must secretly desire it. "Sucked" is a very powerful word. Somehow the word "toaster" makes me think of a woman's genitals in the context of this cartoon.

Sherry. The cartoon, "Lucille was *secretly* thrilled when Norman sucked her toaster," suggests the sexual denial women often indulge in. She (Lucille) certainly is not pictured in a sexy manner, but yet we are informed she is "turned on" by Norman's behavior.

Sid. The Norman here is trying to take in nourishment from the vagina-like toaster. Toasters get hot, and for Lucille this is a hot scene, but that is just precisely why we are able to laugh: because the fantasy is so removed from the probable (toaster as a sex object) that identification by the reader becomes hardly possible; and thus Norman and Lucille are reduced to dehumanized parodies of themselves.

Sophie. Cartoons are very visual . . . we look to see the joke. Like children spying on the adult world, however, we do not always understand what we see. We lack the proper perspective or the proper knowledge. This, I think is why ["Lucille"] does not work for me. I am baffled by these strange (adult) emotions, and fear there must be some dirty pun I am missing.

With all these various responses sorted out into the grid, there are two quite different ways we could compare them. We could go through from top to bottom or from side to side. If we go through from top to bottom, we compare responses by different laughers to a given cartoon. We would ask, presumably, "What do all the responses to that cartoon have in common?" This, in effect, is what those theorists of laughter who talk about the "stimulus" or the "conditions" for laughter have asked.

The conditions theorists looked at a great many occasions of laughter. They asked what the laughings had in common and what the failures to laugh had in common. They came up with suddenness (or the lack of it) and playfulness (or the lack of it). They found their answers not in the laughers, but in the conditions surrounding the laughing.

Similarly, the stimulus theorists looked at many responses, then at the jokes and cartoons that gave rise to those responses. They found—I'm not sure how, given the variability we have seen in this chapter's responses—a single thread running through all the jokes and cartoons that amuse which could be called the stimulus to laughter: incongruity, usually. In practice, I think these stimulus theorists have not resorted to grids. They have simply considered (from an armchair, as it were) a great many occasions of laughter and found similar properties in all the stimuli. The difficulty is that in focusing on just the end of the response, physiological laughter (and indeed usually ignoring the people who don't find the stimulus funny), one loses track of the considerable variation in the thought processes of the laughers.

Some psychologists of laughter have also looked at the matrix from top to bottom, comparing many different laughers' responses, but drawing conclusions about the laughers rather than the cartoon. They have compared one laugher at a cartoon with another, assuming that what you laugh at says something about the kind of person you are. They then find some trait the laughers at a given cartoon have in common that nonlaughers do not.

From this psychological point of view, they might have noticed how Sherry brings in feminist themes where they seem (to me, at least) only distantly relevant. They might point to Sabrina's tendency to treat events as masking gross bodily realities. They might pick up Serge's puncturing of external authorities or his own assumptions. From a more sociological point of view, they might have noticed that a majority of these laughers in 1978 concerned themselves with feminist issues.

Whether their viewpoints are psychological or sociological, the experimenters go on to compare the properties they attribute to the cartoon with the trait in the person responding to it. They would notice Kliban's authority figures, presidents, the clergy, doctors, in connection with Serge's interest in authority or Sabrina's wish to unmask superficials and get down to earthy fundamentals. Often, I think, they build on a stimulus theory but allow for some variation in the response. They are assuming that anyone with the same trait is likely to respond more or less the same way, hence that we laugh according to the category we fall into. They aren't really asking how each individual responds.

Thinking of one person trait by trait may be an attempt to divide what is not divisible. Perhaps the psychologists are setting up categories with edges that will not hold. Trait explanations lose, in any case, the detail and subtlety of the response as a whole.

Here, moreover, we have seen that Sabrina's application of feminist themes differs from Sherry's. Serge's concern with authority leads to responses different from Sid's. We may need something considerably finer than such categories as "feminism" and "concern with authority."

I want a way to talk about the whole response as a whole and its details as details, even if we have to sacrifice the ability, so dear to the experimental mind, to count things. I think we need to be able to think systematically and rigorously about these responses without ignoring the individuality (literally, the undividability) of humans and such human actions as laughing. In order to ask, then, "Why does *one* laugh?" we need some way of thinking systematically about that which is not systematic: human individuality.

9 *Identity*

While studying people's reading, I found a way of speaking about individuals systematically. I found I could understand the way different readings of different texts nevertheless stem from and express the wholeness of one changing and unchanging individual. I could talk about the individual by means of a theory of identity, not quite in Erik Erikson's sense (which is really a sense of identity, an inner feeling of sameness and continuity), but in Heinz Lichtenstein's: identity as a way of thinking about the sameness and difference in a person's behavior.[1] I now think I can apply that way of understanding people's responses to stories and poems to their responses to jokes and humor, in other words, to laughter and the comic.

We perceive both ourselves and others as continuing beings despite drastic changes. In a way, as Murray Schwartz has remarked, that is the nub of the riddle the Sphinx asked Oedipus. What walks on four legs in the morning, two legs at noon, and three legs in the evening—and *is the same being*? The mystery is not change alone, but change in the midst of constancy and constancy in the midst of change.

Everything you or I do is something new, yet we put a personal stamp on everything we do. Everything we do thus has something different about it, but also something that is the same as what we did before. It is only because you can see me as a continuing "I" with a distinct personal style that you can understand a change in me as a change. Conversely, I can discover the sameness in what you do only by seeing what persists through change. We see difference by means of a background of sameness. We see sameness as that which continues through difference. To see either, we need the other.

Lichtenstein has suggested that one can grasp this dialectic of sameness and difference in our personalities through a concept of identity as a theme and variations on that theme. By an identity theme, I mean the sameness or the style that I can trace in someone (or myself) persisting through all the changes. I can then understand the changes and differences as variations on that theme. Of course, just as in a musical theme and variations, I never hear the theme itself in any absolute, Platonic sense, only in some particular embodiment, some variation with a particular timbre, tempo, tone, pitch, speed, and so on. Each musical phrase I hear is new but it is also part of something continuous with the past. One understands the parts of the composition by considering the whole; one learns about the whole through its parts.

To the extent that I can trace in someone's choices in living (as in the choices of a composer) patterns of repetition and contrast, sameness and change, style and content, I can arrive at an identity theme for someone. I can then (perhaps) understand that person's reactions to some new experience, such as Kliban's cartoons, as variations on that theme. I can think of the whole person in all his or her history—the person's identity—as the theme plus all the variations, the whole composition.

To be sure, some things people do will show individuality more than others. I can relate a person's choice of words in a story more richly and densely to identity than that person's answers to a true-false questionnaire or a 0–4 scale of amusement. But I would not start from the assumption that some parts have nothing at all to do with identity any more than I would start listening to a string quartet with the assumption that some parts have nothing to do with the theme of the whole.

Themes are ways to discover a unity, and unless one decides to look for a unity, one will not find it. Even then, of course, one may not. The only sensible way I know to conclude that a given poem or person lacks unity is to assume that there is unity and defeat the assumption. And even then one is trying to prove a negative. Somebody else could always find a way of unifying the poem or the person.

Thus this kind of understanding differs radically from the experimental psychologist's comparisons among many people's responses. This is a *holistic* explanation. It tries to describe one human being as an individual, unique and whole. It accents the ways the person maintains individuality through rules, goals, values, defensive or adaptive strategies, boundary-maintaining techniques, or means for exchange and boundary crossing.[2]

Though holistic analysis is a less familiar method than experiment and correlation, a number of sciences nevertheless draw on it, particularly to frame hypotheses. As I write, for example, physicists are busily trying to reduce the bewildering variety of subatomic particles into a few principles (I would say "themes"), such as three kinds of quark. Usually the scientist can translate such an explanatory principle into an if–then hypothesis on which to base predictions and experiments. But not always. Sometimes conditions rule out experimentation and the scientist does what a psychoanalyst would do: look for more data with which to confirm or defeat a pattern (or thematic) explanation.

Thus one of the great discoveries of recent years, the validation of Alfred Wegener's theory of continental drift, cannot be tested by experiment. Any child can see on a globe that the horn of South America will fit into the bend in the west coast of Africa, but to prove by experiment that they were once joined, the scientist would have to slide continents about and see whether their movement would heave up Himalayas. Instead, for this holistic explanation, one looks for more data. Finding that the positions of shorelines and mountains can be

explained by the movement of continents, scientists looked into suboceanic rocks for a record of shifts in the magnetic pole
that would date such movements. They studied existing "hot
spots" where magma is being pushed upward between continents. They compared the animals of different continents to
establish dates when all our continents were joined into one
huge land mass and then drifted apart. In holistic thinking,
testing takes the form of getting new data that will converge
around the hypothesis or "theme" being tested.

Research on laughter can take a holistic form as well. Identity theory provides an alternative to the usual psychological
search for correlations between trait and trait or between trait
and behavior. In that quest a psychologist usually gives a certain stimulus to a lot of people and so acquires a matrix (as we
did) of jokes or cartoons along one axis, responders along the
other, and laughter (or nonlaughter) at the intersections. In
conventional research, a psychologist tries to separate the traits
that lead to laughter from the traits that don't. The psychologist looks into the matrix from the stimulus side, perhaps
through many cartoons (how do those that get lots of laughs
differ from those that bomb?), perhaps through one (how do
the people who laugh at it differ from the ones who don't?).

With a concept of identity, however, you can peer along the
other edge, the response. You look into the matrix through one
person: how does this person respond to these different cartoons and jokes? You can understand the samenesses and differences in one person's laughings through a centering identity
theme. The differences come as that person transacts different
jokes—as indeed the builders of psychological tests assumed
when they thought they could get at personalities by finding
out what people think is funny. They tried to generalize from
individual to individual too soon, however, before they had
fully worked through one laugher laughing.

When we deal with the personalities of laughers laughing,
then, instead of trying to generalize about many individuals
laughing at the same cartoons, we can generalize about one

individual laughing at many cartoons. A properly scientific researcher needs to generalize over many cases, but they do not cease being "many" just because they all take place within the life of a single human being[3]—or, in the discovery of continental drift, in the history of one planet's land masses.

Freud pictured holistic reasoning as the working of a jigsaw puzzle:

> If one succeeds in arranging the confused heap of fragments, each of which bears upon it an unintelligible piece of drawing, so that the picture acquires a meaning, so that there is no gap anywhere in the design and so that the whole fits into the frame—if all these conditions are fulfilled, then one knows that one has solved the puzzle and that there is no alternative solution.[4]

As early as 1896 he compared this kind of convergence thinking with that of an archaeologist confronted with half-buried ruins, fragments of inscriptions, and the garbled traditions of the local inhabitants. His task is to dig out as many additional data as he can and make them converge into a reading.

> If his work is crowned with success, the discoveries are self-explanatory: the ruined walls are part of the ramparts of a palace or a treasure-house; the fragments of columns can be filled out into a temple; the numerous inscriptions . . . [may] yield undreamed-of information about the events of the remote past, to commemorate which the monuments were built. *Saxa loquuntur!*[5]

This is the *Aha!* experience of psychoanalytic interpretation, the feeling that suddenly all the data are so unified that it is as though mute stones have spoken (although, of course, it is the all-too-loquacious dyad of analyst and analysand that does the talking).

We reason the same way in more commonplace situations, such as figuring out the function of an unknown device. Once I know that this conglomeration of handle, clamp, socket, and plunger is a cherry pitter, I understand that the clamp holds the device to a table; the hemispherical socket holds the cherry;

the plunger pushes the stone through the hole in the socket; the handle pushes the plunger; the slide supplies cherries, and so on. In short, once I have grasped the central theme of pitting cherries, I can use it to relate a host of otherwise baffling details. If the machine is truly functional, one theme will relate all its details. If it is not, if it is something like a combination toothbrush, shoehorn, and bottle opener, the effect can be faintly comic.

We play with this same kind of reasoning in detective stories. "My attention was speedily drawn," explains the immortal Sherlock Holmes at the end of "The Adventure of the Speckled Band,"

> to this ventilator [which ran not to the outer air, but to the adjoining room of the victim's stepfather], and to the bell-rope which hung down to the bed. The discovery that this was a dummy, and that the bed was clamped to the floor, instantly gave rise to the suspicion that the rope was there as a bridge for something passing through the hole and coming to the bed. The idea of a snake instantly occurred to me, and when I coupled it with my knowledge that the doctor was furnished with a supply of creatures from India . . .

Holmes's centering idea, that the doctor was slipping a poisonous snake through the ventilator into his stepdaughter's bed to kill her for her inheritance, interrelates all the details of the story: the positions of the bedrooms, ventilator, and clamped bed *and* the existence of a dummy bell-rope *and* the marks on the chair indicating that someone habitually stood on it *and* the presence of a fine noose, a saucer of milk, and an iron safe (for handling and keeping the snake) *and* whistles heard in the night (summoning it) *and* finally the victim's agonized cry, "The speckled band!" (the snake's appearance). All converge toward Holmes's solution.

Throughout the stories, Holmes demonstrates over and over again this basic strategy of holistic reasoning: bringing clusters of details into mutual relevance around themes. Holmes also demonstrates—handsomely—two criteria for judging the valid-

ity of a holistic explanation: coverage and directness. At first
Holmes entertained a less viperous explanation:

> When you combine the idea of whistles at night, the presence
> of a band of gypsies who are on intimate terms with this old
> doctor, the fact that we have every reason to believe that the
> doctor has an interest in preventing his stepdaughter's mar-
> riage, the dying allusion to a band, and finally, the fact that
> Miss Helen Stoner [the surviving sister] heard a metallic clang,
> which might have been caused by one of those metal bars which
> secured the shutters falling back into their place, I think there is
> good ground to think that the mystery may be cleared along
> those lines.

The pattern of reasoning is the same, converging details toward a centering theme: the doctor somehow let the gypsy
band through the shutters to do the sister in. That would interrelate the whistle, the clang, the presence of gypsies, the doctor's finances, and a dying cry about a "band." But having
arrived at the ingenious idea of the swamp adder, Holmes
comments on the earlier hypothesis: "'I had,' said he, 'come
to an entirely erroneous conclusion, which shows, my dear
Watson, how dangerous it always is to reason from insufficient
data.'"

"Insufficient." One can compare two holistic interpretations
quantitatively, according to the number of details they relate.
Holmes's swamp adder accounts for much more than the gypsy
hypothesis: the ventilator linking the two rooms, the dummy
bell-rope, and the heel-marked chair.

Second, a holistic explanation that relates the details it covers
neatly and directly will usually satisfy us more than one that
establishes only tenuous or devious connections. Holmes's
gypsy explanation does not say how the gypsies murdered the
sister. It simply says "the band" did something. The second
explanation, however, explains "the *speckled* band" exactly as
the appearance of the snake, and "the metallic clang heard by
Miss Stoner was obviously caused by her father hastily closing
the door of his safe upon its terrible occupant."

Holmes demonstrates a third characteristic of holistic reasoning, reliance on particulars instead of categories. The category
"poisonous snake" does not account for as many details as
the more particular "swamp adder" (poisonous plus speckled).
Similarly, Holmes explains better when he deals with the dying
sister's exact words, " 'The speckled band!' " Categories even
more general explain even less, like the biblical conclusion
Holmes draws at the end: "Violence does, in truth, recoil upon
the violent, and the schemer falls into the pit which he digs for
another."

Because of this need for particulars, holistic research does
not proceed by counting or by repeating experiments but by
gathering more data. Holmes has to visit Stoke Moran, where,
having surmised that the ventilator ran from the victim's room
to the doctor's, he can now see its size and position, find an
iron safe, and discover that the victim's bed is clamped to the
floor. Research leads to more data, which ask for a stronger
explanation, one that leaves no loose ends in this now larger
body of material.

"No loose ends" is an aesthetic criterion. While this kind of
thinking-toward-wholeness is only one of several methods in
the sciences, it dominates systematic thought in the arts and
humanities. I find it striking how exactly the social scientist's
holistic analysis (or "pattern explanation") corresponds to the
orthodox method of the literary critic. René Wellek calls it "the
main source of knowledge in all humanistic branches of learning, from theology to jurisprudence, from philology to the history of literature. It is a process that has been called 'the circle
of understanding.' It proceeds from attention to a detail to an
anticipation of the whole and back again to an interpretation of
a detail."[6] Someone analyzing (as opposed to evaluating or "responding to") a poem or a fiction (or a painting or a symphony)
usually proceeds in the same way as the archaeologist, the
anthropologist, the clinical psychologist, or Holmes. One no-
tices patterns of recurrence or absence. One articulates them as
different themes, checking them against the evidence and fit-

ting them together to form a model of a whole consisting of an inferred theme (a theme of themes) at the center and a surface of subthemes and variations.

As a literary critic I would ask that the theme and subthemes let me bring under them every detail of the text I am analyzing and, if there be a central "theme of themes," that I be able to bring all the lesser themes under it. I think of a holistic analysis of a literary text as the creation of ladders of abstractions such that I can at least try to trace any one detail, even the tiniest, up one or another ladder to the very center. Conversely I think of the central theme as a kernel statement each one of whose terms I can expand, transform, and particularize until I arrive back out at the details of the text I am working with. A holistic analysis lets me work systematically with a text but still be faithful to its details and its uniqueness.

I can *work with* the text. Obviously, someone who wants to analyze a poem or a person holistically must, like a doctor or a psychiatrist, form a relationship with it, simultaneously observing and participating in both the system's routines and its crises. One cannot simply set up a holistic analysis like an experiment and "let it run." One must be actively, energetically, and empathically engaged at every stage of interpreting and inferring, like a cultural anthropologist, a literary critic, a psychoanalyst, or a Sherlock Holmes.

To formulate someone's identity (in my usage of the term, following and particularizing Lichtenstein's), I employ this kind of holistic analysis or pattern explanation to explore a personality. I infer themes from the details of a person's actions, words, and thoughts. I bring those themes together (as best I can) toward a central theme that may embrace them all.

There are two different ways of thinking about that theme. Lichtenstein speaks of a "primary identity" that an infant develops in the course of being the child for this particular mother (with her identity). The infant acquires its own primary identity, a zero point that constitutes what the child brings to all future experiences. Lichtenstein thinks of this primary identity as something imprinted and "in" the child. To be sure, one can never fully know it, for, having been formed before speech, it is preverbal. One can never put it exactly into words, although it helps clarify one's inferences to try. One can know it only by inference. Nevertheless, according to Lichtenstein, a primary identity is "there," "in" the person, and you can see, in videotapes of mothers and babies, how the exchange of glances, the ballet of the spoon, or the struggle of the bath constitutes a dialogue. The baby is the baby *for* this particular mother. The baby calls forth the style of the mother, and the mother calls forth the emerging style of the baby.

Although I have seen such videotapes, I believe one need not be so stringent. I prefer to think instead of an "identity theme" that is a constancy I (or someone else) infers about that child or adult after it has developed. An identity theme, in this strict sense, is not "in" a person, but "in" your or my interpretation of that person. It is a part of a relationship, an identity-finding relationship.

An identity theme in this second sense does not try to formulate someone, pinned and wriggling on the paper. It is a way of asking about that person, a hypothesis open to correction as the individual creates further evidence in the course of living. In a way, an identity theme makes no more than the opening statement in an explanatory conversation. To formulate an identity theme is to ask for feedback and dialogue.

That is why I think it is so important to put an identity theme (or "primary identity") into words. Neither I nor anyone else will finally settle *the* meaning of "The Love Song of J. Alfred Prufrock," yet that is all the more reason for me to phrase my own interpretation as carefully as I can. If I do not frame my hypothesis, how can I change it? How engage in that feedback, sharing evidence and comparing interpretations, without which one can only memorize received truths? I don't want to be like the student in the back row who never raises his hand.

Philosophers use the term "explanatory commitment" to

say I have to invest myself emotionally in my interpretation in order to develop it intellectually. One way—there may be others, of course—to make that commitment to an identity theme (or a primary identity) is to state a "theme of themes" as faithfully as one can to cover all the themes and details one is trying to include.

As a practical matter, one infers an identity theme and a primary identity the same way, and one would use the same wording for each. They entail, however, different understandings of the dynamics of the person. An identity theme is simply my inference about someone. If I believe in a primary identity, however, I am claiming that I have discovered something in the person which is active, like other structures posited by psychoanalysts (an ego and an id, for example).

Indeed, Lichtenstein proposed his concept of identity and an "identity principle" as a more explanatory interpretation of what lies "beyond the pleasure principle" than Freud's death instinct (also something "in" the person). Freud's clinical experience led him to a two-level theory of motivation. First, the basic, deep motivation was the pleasure principle: we act so as to avoid unpleasure. Second, as we develop from infancy, we learn to modify and delay our demands for pleasure and to adjust them to reality so as to obtain a greater net pleasure. We acquire a reality principle that supplements and modifies the pleasure principle.

By 1923, however, several phenomena had convinced Freud that something "beyond the pleasure principle" was needed to explain human behavior. People who experienced shocks in accidents or battle would repeat the trauma in dreams. Patients showed a "negative therapeutic reaction." That is, insight alone was not enough. The patients had to take the time to "work through" what they had learned. Freud began to encounter whole character neuroses: our all-too-human tendency to create the same neurotic mess over and over, no matter how painful.

To explain these actions that ran counter to the pleasure

principle, Freud introduced the idea of a compulsion to repeat. The human (and any other) organism tends to try again the solution to an inner or outer demand that has worked before, whether or not it is the best solution under new circumstances. Freud called it the "inertia" or the "conservatism" in human motives.

Freud went on, however, to suggest that the repetition compulsion might simply represent one aspect of something much larger, a tendency for all living matter to try to return to an earlier, inorganic state, free of disturbing stimulation—in short, to die. He called it the "death instinct."

Lichtenstein suggests an alternative to Freud's admittedly speculative and tentative hypothesis. He proposes that the deepest layer of motivation "beyond the pleasure principle" is an "identity principle": a human must maintain identity. The human (or any other) organism seeks to fulfill the law of its being, whatever defines it as what it is: identity. Once an organism has begun to be, as we say, "not itself," it decays and dies. Thus something defines what the organism is, and that something defines what is its pleasure and indeed its reality.

For an elm or a frog, biology substantially defines the law of its being. All elms or frogs will have (from our point of view) the same needs, desires, and connections with the world, at least as far as we humans can say. When we look at our fellow humans, however, we find identities far more individual.

According to Lichtenstein, a person's identity comes from his or her individual history. Lichtenstein follows the English psychoanalytic school in giving great importance to the baby's relation with its "primary caretaker" (in present-day Western culture, its mother). The mother creates a baby, but the baby creates a mother. Between them they form a "potential space" in which the baby shapes its inherited being to become that baby who fits the unconscious needs (or identity) of this particular mother. In effect, says Lichtenstein, the mother imprints a primary identity, a theme, on which all subsequent life plays variations and variations on variations.

The developing child brings that primary identity to all subsequent events. Training, gender, culture, the Oedipus complex, adolescence—all pose tasks or, if you will, questions. The child hears them in its particular style and answers in that style, acting and behaving and so developing further that style and identity. Every second brings new actions, but we can trace a sameness, a personal style, in each new action. Thus an identity principle will explain the repetitions and constancies Freud was trying to explain with the death instinct, but it will do so through precise details of behavior, far less metaphysically or mystically.

Lichtenstein asserts an identity principle based on a "primary identity" within the person. I believe, however, I need not and perhaps cannot claim so much. I need not claim that my inference of an "identity theme" has located a "primary identity" in you. I can simply say that my inferences are consistent with the idea of an identity principle as the deepest motivation on which both the pleasure and the reality principles rest. I can never know that deepest motivation or, indeed, know that there is such a thing—only that my observations fit that hypothesis.

The individual is free under either hypothesis, however. If I assume that someone really has a primary identity inside and that my inferences have approximated it, then the individual is free in the sense that philosophers say people are free in a world of physical causality. That is, Lichtenstein's idea of a primary identity fits within Kant's idea of human freedom (in the *Critique of Practical Judgment*): we are free, even if we live out an *inner* necessity, so long as we do not suffer an *outer* compulsion.

If, however, one takes the easier hypothesis, simply that one can read a person's behavior as though there were a centering identity theme, then, of course, my inferring a style for you does not limit your freedom. My observations and inferences, be they all-covering and direct or not, cannot affect, in and of themselves, what you choose, any more than my taking your temperature can give you a fever.

Rather, your choices lead me to alter my inferences. A dras-

tic, unexpected act requires me to rewrite my hypothesis, because the phrasing of an identity theme asks for feedback.
Under either hypothesis, then, primary identity or identity
theme, we are free to recreate ourselves.

Identity thus promises an explanation of laughter flexible
enough to admit our personal wills. Shown some Kliban cartoons, we can laugh—or we may not find them funny. We can
like one cartoon and not another. We can interest ourselves in
this detail or that. And we can respond differently at different
times. Identity theory offers us a systematic way of understanding laughers laughing which has criteria for strong and weak
explanations; which deals with details of both joke and response; which will allow for cultural and biological influences;
which acknowledges the possibility of psychic determinism yet
does not violate our human feeling that we are free to choose
as we like. To use identity theory, however, we need to go
beyond Chapter 8's quick scanning of responses. We need to
listen at length to one laugher laughing and telling us about it.

10 *Why Ellen Laughed*

There are so many explanations of why we laugh. Consider the King Kong cartoon on the following page. There are incongruities: between the fantastic world of King Kong and this humdrum diner; between what New York ought to have done with that gigantic body lying at the foot of the Empire State Building (or World Trade Center, according to the remake) and what evidently was done; between these "little" people in the diner and the fantastic, fabulous, mythic ape; and there must be dozens more. There is an arousal jag, the sudden solving of the riddle posed by the caption and the equally sudden realization that it is all playful foolery. There is a sense of superiority: these mere mortals have killed and eaten the monstrous ape. There is aggression—against Kong, but also against these victimized consumers. There is even an archetype: the sacramental eating of the slain god.

There are so many explanations of why we laugh, and they succeed too well. That is, they all deliver explanations even when they are inconsistent with one another. For instance, the eating of King Kong is both sacred and disgusting. The diners are both superior and inferior to Kong. Moreover, the theories won't explain why some people are not amused (except for the condition theories: the joke wasn't sudden enough or didn't create a suffcent frame of playfulness).

Instead of generalizing about many laughers or seeking a common denominator in all the various occasions on which

143

@. WHAT DID THE CITY OF NEW YORK DO WITH KING KONG?

people laugh, I would like to start with a single person's laughing. The person in question I shall call Ellen.

This is what she said about the King Kong cartoon:

> The thing that attracted me to the [Kliban] book, if you want to know, the thing I like best—about my favorite drawing, at first, was the guy eating the hamburger, "What did the City of New York do with King Kong?" . . . That was so perfect—because I've eaten there.

Now what does her feeling that she has eaten in that kind of diner have to do with her laughing at this cartoon?

So far as I know, no theorist of humor has ever asked just that sort of question before. In all my scrabbling among ancient and modern theories of laughter, I have never found a detailed case study of one laugher laughing.

Ellen, however, was—is—more of a friend than a case. I had known her for just about three years at the time of our interview about laughter. Having read some writings and lectures by "the Buffalo school," she applied as a graduate student in literature and psychology to the State University of New York at Buffalo. She arrived in the fall of 1975, and, as it happened, she roomed with a woman who had been a friend of my wife's and mine for many years. Thus Ellen began as a student but soon became a friend as well. From time to time the four of us would have dinner or meet before or after a movie. During that first year Ellen had to endure the fatal cancer of someone close to her, whom I also knew, but less well than she did. Ellen held on with devotion and fortitude, and the experience added yet another dimension to our relationship. From 1976 through 1978, Ellen took more seminars in the literature and psychology program associated with our Center for the Psychological Study of the Arts, and eventually she wrote her dissertation with us. It was in January 1978 that I asked her if she would give me an interview about the cartoons of B. Kliban.

I chose Kliban partly because Ellen liked him so much—she had given my wife and me a copy of *Never Eat Anything Bigger than Your Head & Other Drawings* as a house present. Partly I chose him because he seemed to pose the problem of laughter so precisely. That is, Ellen, I, and many others find him hilariously funny. Lots of people, however, like some of the subjects of Chapter 8, find him not only unfunny but positively repellent.

I asked Ellen partly because she herself has such a rich sense of humor. Among our flock of graduate students, she had become a leavening spirit, chief designer of posters, in-jokes, imitations, funny gossip, and even a "prom" for faculty and students. In fact, she herself has published a satirical essay on the theme of graduate students being paid to read books. Thus I, the assiduous theorist of the comic, could compare the style of Ellen's own comic writing with Kliban's to see if they meshed.

There was another reason I asked Ellen. I knew her in a rather special way, apart from her writings, our friendship, and her experiences while a graduate student in our program at the State University of New York at Buffalo. In the fall of

1975 (at the time she was coping with the death of our mutual friend), she had taken part in one of our "Delphi" seminars. In these seminars, we try to achieve for each participant a sense of the personal style he or she brings to literary transactions, be they criticism, teaching, or simply reading. The members of the seminar circulate to one another open free-associative responses to literary texts. Then, part way through the semester, the group takes these open responses as themselves the texts to respond to.[1] Hence I had my own and several others' interpretations of Ellen's style of reading. I would be able to conceptualize Ellen's response through readings of her personal style—her identity—by all the members of the seminar, including Ellen herself.

Writing now—and trying to be concise—I would state my 1975 interpretation of Ellen's theme this way: I give of myself so that a self will give to me. Stating that early interpretation, I feel rather embarrassed, it is so abstruse and laconic. To be sure, I can plead that the seminar had asked me to do an exemplary analysis, studied and formal, of an identity theme, but even so . . . At any rate, I wrote a 2,000-word analysis, quoting many examples from her writings and finally suggesting as the core of Ellen's style: "to give and so turn the 'other' from a missed to an imagined to a giving humanity."

Again, I am not trying to fix Ellen in a formulated phrase like J. Alfred Prufrock sprawling on a pin. The reason I quite carefully put an identity theme into words is precisely to give the seminar something to debate and me something to change in the light of her later actions. Were Ellen before me now, such an "identity theme" could be the start of a discussion that would add to the words from which I would infer her identity theme.

Writing Ellen into a book is like taking her snapshot and putting it in an album. This identity theme preserves her as I saw her in 1975, so that my use of my 1975 reading of Ellen is a way of assuring you that I did not "read" her solely in terms of her response to Kliban. The fixity, regrettable in one way, in another provides a stable point of view from which to assay her laughing in 1978.

I now find those 1975 thematic terms annoyingly abstract, however. I want to flesh them out by drawing on themes others talked about as well as my own unfoldings at the time. For example, *the other*: it seemed to me that Ellen posited a world polarized into dualities, particularly the dualism of self and other. Others in the seminar wrote: "'Between Two Worlds' seems to be your theme . . . an attempt to straddle both worlds at once." "Many times in your responses you speak of existing between, or being torn between, two positions."

Ellen, I thought, conceived of that separated other primarily as a source (rather than, as someone else might, a threat or a promise). The other was a superior being who might give her something or whom Ellen might become. According to one seminar member, Ellen imagined merger with a "great mystical food; body with immense power beneath the surface; great life force; another world." Ellen was much, much interested in food.

If she *missed* the other, that would pose a considerable risk, even (in fantasy) starvation. As she said of herself, "Separation is sometimes so painful for me that I cannot bear the loss." Ellen tried therefore to constitute that other being, to make sure it was really there, and then not to be cut off from it.

She would ensure the other's giving to her by her own giving. She said of herself, "I enjoy giving gifts and also receiving them." A seminar member expanded on a sentence Ellen had written about Sylvia Plath: "'The woman performs an exchange and thereby benefits.' You give your mother [feigned illness], she gives you love. You give teachers insightful analysis, they give you praise. . . . [Then] you re-imagine the exchange as giving." That is, Ellen gives in order to receive, but *re-imagines* a this-for-that exchange as altruistic giving.

She imagines the other to be a freely bountiful source. To make it so, Ellen gives food and belief, but most interestingly, intelligence, work, wit, imagination, and even play-acting (as when she played sick for her mother: "A lie can produce maternal love," one student interpreted). I thought I saw in this playful giving the way Ellen's own joking and laughing fulfilled a cluster of deep needs. That is, Ellen sought to transform the *missed* other by *giving* and being given to. Her wit was one important way she gave.

Ellen fitted what others said about her into this pattern of needed giving. She wrote, "I take very seriously what others say about me, having little confidence in my own opinions. I am most susceptible to suggestion." Another student agreed: "You often berate yourself, don't quite trust yourself." It was as though, by giving up something good about herself, Ellen would ensure that someone would give something good back to her.

In trying to word all these traits as a theme, I was (characteristically) abstract: "to give and so turn the other from a missed to an imagined to a giving humanity." And, of course, in giving her that formal analysis, I was fulfilling her identity. She had given of herself (in the seminar) so that another self—I or the other individuals in the seminar—would give to her.

The ideas of the others in the seminar help me give body to my own abstract words. They do not, however, imply consensus or that Ellen "has" some identity theme on which skillful interpreters agree. Rather, all of us in the 1975 seminar were inquiring together into her feelings and associations, constituting her identity and our own by that very act. Since my thinking about her identity is itself a part of my own identity, I contributed to our data just as she did. Confirmation of my interpretation—my feeling that I was directly, neatly interrelating many details of what Ellen said—took place as she and I talked then and later.

We held our interview on January 31, 1978. I had asked Ellen if she would talk about her amusement at Kliban, explaining as best she could what she found funny and also free-associating. I didn't, obviously, expect Ellen to explain what hundreds of other theorists, starting with Aristotle, had already overexplained. I did expect her to express ideas, images, associations, and feelings from which I could infer something about her mental processes. Nothing, of course, could recapture her lightning-fast sense of being amused the first time she saw the cartoon. But I expected our interview to make it possible for me to establish a continuity between her amusement *during the interview* at the cartoon and her previous amusement and, indeed, many other actions in her life, functions of her identity as I understood it.

We talked into a tape recorder for about an hour, paging back and forth through *Never Eat Anything Bigger than Your Head*. I have transcribed our speech hesitations, broken sentences, slang and all, tidying up only slightly for the printed page the messiness one always finds in spoken language. Rather than simply reproduce the interview, however, I can present a more coherent reading if I report segments of our conversation according to themes. In the text of this chapter, I'll analyze Ellen's response, and in the accompanying boxes I'll reproduce her words as I analyze them.

Incidentally, understanding Ellen's amusement by means of identity does not rule out the traditional theories of laughter (although, as we shall see, they acquire a new context). On the contrary, a large part of Ellen's laughter answered very neatly to the incongruity theories, for example, her response to the crowning of Cynthia. She saw this cartoon as an example of a general pattern, which (she said) was one big source of the book's appeal to her. We would call it a Platonic or ethical incongruity. Ellen said the Cynthia cartoon set the low or mundane world of groceries next to the "high" world of the pope or the king of Norway. Another cartoon (accurately captioned "Dirty Fat Person Sits on President's Face") she called "the wedding of the arcane and the sublime . . . complete raunch with what shouldn't be raunch—like here: 'Our Founder,'" she said, pointing to the facing cartoon, a statue inscribed "Our Founder": a man in a business suit with a huge erection bulging in his pants.

"Cynthia Is Mistakenly Crowned King of Norway"

ELLEN. One of the things about this book I really like is . . . they take just totally mundane things and take something really high, put it next to it, and—I mean, the caption makes the story, and also she's carrying groceries and they mistakenly crown her king of Norway. . . . That they should take the entire . . . apparatus—and it looks like the pope or some archbishop or something—walking down the middle of the street and find this lady carrying groceries and mistakenly crown her king of Norway. You wonder who they were looking for.

"Lucille Was Secretly Thrilled . . ."

ELLEN. "Lucille was secretly thrilled when Norman sucked her toaster." I don't know if you identify with this or not . . .

NNH. No [laughing]. No, I don't identify with that Norman. No.

ELLEN. But I'm always amazed by what I assume this is, a sexual perversion. . . . You just kind of stare at it, and you know it's hysterically funny—and that's the feeling I have in general about sexual perversions. You feel like you should understand them because they're human, but you just don't know what makes people get off on them . . . you don't know—but you just want to know. And the idea that somebody can really get turned on while someone else sucks a toaster. I mean, he really is in position here, and she's not completely dressed . . . [She's] built like the Shetland House ladies [a local bar], I mean, she has curlers in her hair, and it's so mundane.

NNH. Is "mundane" the word you want? "Gross," isn't it?

ELLEN. It's gross, but it's also mundane. It's very Monday morning. It's beyond mundane. . . . You can see the plug, the toaster—this is a particular brand of toaster. You know, the kind that comes up like that? It's brown?

Of Lucille and Norman and the toaster, she said, "This is terrific. I like this a lot." She talked about perversion. One ought to be able to understand other people's perversions, she said, out of common humanity, but she couldn't figure them

out, and they ended up funny. What interested me was that
Ellen took Kliban's unreal, almost surreal cartoon and tried to
think about it as if it were real, like Cynthia's shopping for
groceries. She went on to compare Lucille with women she had
seen in a local bar—realism again. She pinpointed the toaster
as a particular brand. It was all, she said, "very Monday morning," very mundane and ordinary. But, as she herself acknowl-
edged, the cartoon points to an utterly bizarre perversion.

No term as abstract as "incongruity" quite does justice to the
individuality of Ellen's response. She contrasts the mundane,
arcane, raunchy, or gross with the sublime or the high, but
the mere label "incongruous" misses the distinctive quality of
the low side in her contrasts: "this lady carrying groceries,"
"the Shetland House ladies with curlers in their hair," or the
toaster whose manufacturer can be identified. Ellen contrasts
an everyday, here-and-now realism with the pope or "some
archbishop" or the adjective she finds for the president: "sublime." She contrasts something real with something exotic or
out of the ordinary that she has to figure out.

Partly she didn't want to be bothered "figuring." She wanted
the book simply to give her pleasure without any effort on her
part. "What I really like about it [the book] is . . . It's just like
watching TV. You don't have to do anything, and it's not like
me telling a joke. You don't have to remember all the details.
You just look, and it's there."

Kliban captions a lot of his jokes with numbers, as though
they were part of a series: "More Than Coincidence? #9," "House-
hold Hint #161." When we looked at a cartoon labeled "Bizarre
Practices #83," I asked Ellen if she had ever made any sense of
these numbers. "I just figured it was over my head," she said.
"It was beyond me to figure out what number was what."
Again, toward the end of the interview, when I asked, "How
about 'Chapter Eleven'?" (another caption), she answered, "It's
a jokebook. I didn't have to work at it. . . . I also figured that I
wasn't understanding the whole book at once [i.e., as a unity]
because it had numbers, and I never bothered to put them

"Cynthia Is Mistakenly Crowned King of Norway"

ELLEN. She also looks like "Huh?" You know, like "Give me a break!" You know, stuff like this happens to me all the time. I mean, not that they crown me king of Norway, but like you're in the middle of your routine, and something out of the ordinary happens and maybe the whole tone of the book is, "Ah? Aw, give me a break. It's so mundane." That look on her face is better than— Everybody else is just really into crowning her king of Norway.

NNH. And she just looks blank.

ELLEN. Not even blank. Just like "Aw, I'm carrying groceries." She looks like she's either waiting for the car to go by and cross the street or something—she's in the middle of her day—and they— "God damn it, they're crowning me king of Norway again. They make these mistakes all the time."

"Pies of the World"

ELLEN. And you start. "Oh, Argentina. Uh-huh. Greece . . . And Yugoslavia, and uh-huh . . ." You go through and by the time you get to the end, "Did I miss something?" And you go through again. And you realize you spent all this time looking at identical things, and if somebody brought it to your attention— It's kind of like fifth-grade social studies. You have it the whole year and then you find out that the answer to all the questions is: people are people all over the world.

---

together. I never bothered—it's a jokebook. Why should one have to?" Why indeed? (Ans.: Because of *my* identity.)

Ellen imagined the book as giving to her without her having to do anything in return (half of her characteristic wish). "It's not like me telling a joke." Yet this bounty was not altogether comfortable. When crowned king of Norway, her Cynthia swore, "God damn it. Give me a break." Being crowned made an annoying interruption in her routine.

Partly Ellen wanted the cartoons simply to give to her at her convenience, and she structured them into the mutual giving that was central to her identity. Also, however, she would say such things as "You just want to know" and "You should understand them." She was wishing to "figure it out." She described herself thinking about "Dirty Fat Person Sits on President's Face." "I wonder what's funny about it. I wonder what other captions we could put in. . . . I've tried to figure out which is funnier, the captions or the picture." Talking about "Pies of the World," a cartoon showing eight large, lumpy pies, each labeled with the name of a different country, she described herself trying not to miss anything, and she remembered fifth-grade social studies, how she had finally caught on at the end of the year. The pattern I saw was: She would figure something out so that, after passively not knowing at first, she had superior knowledge in the end.

A cartoon she liked was "Victor Grows More Suspicious Hourly." She shaped it into this same characteristic pattern. She began by nudging the cartoon toward a more realistic situation: an old movie, rather than a cartoon. Then she moved to a still more realistic situation, when as a child she had overheard her parents discussing a visit to her school. They forgave her. "It's OK that I'm getting a D in math." And she wondered if they were saying that only because they knew she was listening. Then she began to doubt the reality of "they" entirely. "Do they really have rabbit suits on? Are they really my parents? Am I dreaming this?" She wondered about suspicion, and why Victor only grew suspicious slowly, "which is dumb." Victor is "limited." "Everybody here is pretty dumb."

The joke had many dimensions for Ellen. Are those others really real? Are they as real as a cowboy movie? Are they dressed as bears or as rabbits? By reading rabbits as bears or vice versa, she made the cartoon even more unreal.

Note how she hovered between the unreality of the situation and realistic explanations of it. They are not really bears (or rabbits), just dressed that way. Victor is a lunatic. Victor is dumb.

Are they real and superior beings, like my parents when

"Victor Grows More Suspicious Hourly"

Ellen. It's like an old movie or cowboy movie where they're all plotting, and you see him behind a tree watching it. Only what's so weird is, Victor is a *little* confused. [Laugh] With good reason he should grow suspicious. . . . My association is to my family—to my parents late at night, talking about me. "What do you think? She really did flunk that test?" And I've been straining to hear—like they've come home from open house [at school]. "She's getting a D in math." And I'm listening, and I grow suspicious. It's OK.

NNH. What's OK?

Ellen. It's OK that I'm getting a D in math. . . . And I think there's something wrong. Do they know I'm listening? . . . Do they really have rabbit suits on? Are these really my parents? Am I dreaming this? No wonder I should grow suspicious. They say it's OK. . . . It's a situation that you should be suspicious of, because there are people behaving strangely.

On the other hand, what's even funnier is that suspicion doesn't mean that you're sure. This is a situation where you should be sure there's something wrong going on. He just grows suspicious hourly. It takes a little while. He's only growing suspicious. . . . These are so understated that there's a real distance between what should be going on, what is going on, and what's told—the biggest difference being, Victor is a lunatic because he's not running away from the other lunatics that are dressed up as bears. And he's really just standing behind a tree trying to figure it out, which is dumb. And even further away than that, the narrator tells you how limited he is. . . . A lot of slow people in here. Yeah. Everybody here is pretty dumb.

---

they forgave me? Ellen's Victor is doing just what Ellen does. He is figuring out how to relate to those mysterious beings, but he does it more stupidly than Ellen does, and Ellen can feel superior to him.

Another way Ellen made herself intellectually both inferior and superior, given to and giving, was by finding allusions. As she said, "This is a cartoon book, so it must not be real. But it gives you ideas." Or she it. For example, she treated Norman's sucking the toaster as an allusion to "What's Your Perversion?" in Woody Allen's *Everything You Always Wanted to Know about Sex*. In the same way she saw a cartoon showing a caveman rubbing a stick ("Stick Cleaning Simplified") as an allusion to Mel Brooks's two-thousand-year-old man. "It's like a joke on Rube Goldberg. Instead of taking a complex thing . . . it's got just three figures. This is how you clean a stick. To explain the simple with all kinds of diagrams. It's just absurd." "Arnold Meets Two Other Arnolds" (showing three identically lumpy figures greeting each other) reminded her of "the end of *The Trial*, where . . . those two guys come along." The title cartoon, "Never Eat Anything Bigger than Your Head," she saw as an allusion to Mr. Grimwig in *Oliver Twist*, who kept vowing to "eat my head." Ellen thought that Kliban's first book, *Cats*, was an allusion to *Puss in Boots*.

In general, I thought her many comparisons of the cartoons to stories and books not just a symptom of her being a graduate student, but a way to show her own knowledge or experience. For example, she saw the fly cartoon as "an allusion to another joke. You know the fly jokes." Well, no, I didn't. By her comparisons she showed her own superiority to and control of the materials she was comparing. Perhaps she also showed her superiority to and control of the person she was talking to.

Her comparisons also split the relation between Ellen and the cartoon, as her finding of incongruities did. First there had been the cartoon. Now there was the cartoon plus the thing alluded to. By pointing to allusions, she created two things to relate to where there had been only one.

A whole series of other cartoons enabled Ellen to split or double her relation to "the other." These cartoons were like puzzles in that she felt she had to figure out how to relate herself to them. Hence she could be both intellectually superior and inferior.

One drawing shows a group of identically bland men in hats

ELLEN. This is one that I liked too. "Always Hide in a Place Where There Are a Lot of the Same Things." I love the right-wrong captions. . . . I like giving bad advice and knowing— It takes things out of everyday and warps them.

Y—— and I were putting up posters for the prom last year. We cut one out of a magazine. It was funny. . . . It was an ad for insurance and was a picture of people without faces, indicating on the next page that you would be a face to them [this insurance company], not as these people are to other companies [blanks]. And we hung this picture up and the caption was, "What Is Wrong with This Picture?" As if you wouldn't notice.

It's a satire on the kind of thing that they used to have in Girl Scout magazines, which is, "There are seven rabbits in this picture. Find them." And I diligently do things like that, all the time. I do follow things, and what is right and wrong. I'm a real victim of charts and graphs and pictures.

And the other things that we all satirize now is when we were little girls and we used to get little booklets on menstruation. And they'd say things like, "On these days you will not want to run ay-round a lot. You will sit in a chair and drink tea. You will take baths but not hot baths." And it goes on with this really ridiculous, stupid thing that has since been disproved by normal people, and I mean— Well, any five-year-old could tell you that this is stupid now. But we believed it. And I would see a movie, and they would show a picture of a girl riding a bicycle, and it would say, "Wrong." And beside it, it would show a picture of a girl sitting on a chair reading a book, and it would say, "Right." And I studied it. It was like, I can't get my period until I know this. You know, the fifties sense of "I have to do this, and I have to do it right." . . .

There's right and wrong and I since think about the good little girl that I was and how absurd it was to do these right and wrong things and to look at the pictures and be told and to agree with them. And I love somebody who makes fun of that. You know, your mother says, "If you're a gorilla, and you want to hide, don't go where there aren't other gorillas." "Yes, Mom. OK." I feel so— I've listened to these pictures before.

walking along and, among them, a gorilla. The caption says,
"Always Hide in a Place Where There Are a Lot of the Same
Things." Ellen liked this one particularly. She loved the "right-
wrong captions" (a splitting?). She liked being given bad advice
and then knowing better. It was as though someone warped
her sense of reality, but then she won it back. She liked to
make jokes for other people, using this same "stupid advice"
format. She recalled a poster she had made for the departmen-
tal "prom," a picture of a whole group of people with no faces,
which she captioned, "What Is Wrong with This Picture?" Her
associations then ran to simple-minded puzzles in Girl Scout
magazines, and from there to the advice she had gotten as a
girl on menstruation and taking it easy on "these days." She
laughed at "this really ridiculous, stupid thing that has since
been disproved by normal people. . . . But we believed it."
Indeed, she had felt compelled to study and master it. She
couldn't have her first period, as it were, until she got this
thing right. She said she loved "somebody who makes fun of
that." At the same time, it was real: "I've listened to these
pictures before."

Ellen responded to the gorilla cartoon by supplying givers: a
foolish mother and old-fashioned pamphlets that gave her stupid advice. But then she showed she was superior to the ad-

---

"SHORT ON BRAINS, BUT A TERRIFIC DANCER"

ELLEN. They're the ugliest people I ever saw, and I think I went
to school with a lot of them. . . . "Greasers," we called them.
We went to "mixers" and we met "greasers." We used to have
signals for when you meet people like this. This meant [she
gestured] "Come save me or I'll never speak to you again."
There are people who *look* like this! You know the type: five-
o'clock shadow the year round, all day, and it's very scary.
And a lot of blank looks. I like the really ugly, grotesque,
blank-look people.

vice, and she could outadvise her friends about menstruation or she could enable us to enjoy the same kind of Klibanian joke she does by her feignedly naive poster puzzle or she could enable her professors to be childish by having a "prom." By having been given to, she becomes the giver.

Partly Ellen becomes the recipient of advice by being "a real victim of charts and graphs and pictures." Partly she gets satisfaction by being superior to such ploys, and she showed her sense of superiority in her general remarks about Kliban's characters, especially what she said about the "Short on Brains" cartoon. Kliban's characters are "the ugliest people I ever saw," and she recalled school dances where she would signal a friend to come rescue her from some dreadful "greaser" with "five o'clock shadow" and a "blank look." At other points in the interview, she said such things as "These people are nerds. They all look the same. They're all ugly. . . . I've had students like this, and they are really horribly built people."

Earlier I had asked Ellen why she found it amusing when Kliban took some unpleasant, ugly piece of reality and put it into a cartoon. She answered that Kliban was demonstrating that someone else sees the world in the same "very critical" way she does. Further, she does not perceive the world and then judge it. This is the way she sees it first off, and the fact that Kliban puts ugly things in his cartoons simply proves that "somebody else sees what I see."

> NNH. But why is it funny to take an unpleasant chunk of reality and put it in a cartoon? A grubby, ugly part of reality.
> ELLEN. Because it admits that it's there. That's the best part of it, that you see, I see—I am very critical. [My best friend] tells me that I'm overly critical of people and of things, and I say, "What's the difference between being critical and being discerning?" Apparently the difference is, I'm the only one that discerns in this way, and this book proves that somebody else sees what I see.
> NNH. Sees the world as you see it.
> ELLEN. Yeah.

ELLEN. Why do I like ugliness? Did I finish that?

NNH. Well, you said because it's there. Because it says that it exists.

ELLEN. Because I know people who look like this . . . Carl and Ramon. . . . This is Ramon Navarro. And this is Carl. You know, the scrawlings on the page and his furtive look. Fat. No one's well built in this— Everybody's fat. Everybody's kind of hunchbacked or uneven and— Ugly hair, no one has decent hair. . . . And either they're all completely clean-shaven, which doesn't fit right with the shape of their faces, or they're pockmarked. Their hair is just— I don't know. It's just so ugly, and his hands are stubby, and he's leaning out of the chair. This guy looks so neat, but this guy's got grub all over his suit.

And you see people who look like that, and you look at them, and you say, "Oh, this is so disgusting." And you want to think up words for it, and you want to describe it to someone, and you know if you tell someone, they're going to think you're a horrible person, and in a way it's funny that you see it, and can't say it, and you know that some-body else sees it.

And another way it's frustrating because— Well, it's dis-tancing, too. It's like saying, "I'm not like that. See, I can think of all the words that describe it, and I'm not that." But it's also putting it out there, and it's seeing it. It's seeing difference and— It's also maybe identifying with it a little, getting scared rather than laughing.

But somebody else saw it, and you can put it down, that nobody's hurt for it and that they sell it as a jokebook. What do they do, if this could be entitled, "The Book Which Sent B. Kliban into Prison?"

NNH. I don't know. That wouldn't be funny.

ELLEN. . . . Yeah, I'm into this thing about how I can see things that other people can't. It's a big power trip. . . . Because Y—— keeps telling me that I'm overly demanding, and the last time [I talked to her] I said, "Well, that's it. This is the way I see things." I finally had enough nerve to say, "This is the way I think the world is."

NNH. Oh. You mean like the used-car dealers? [Another set of deformed Kliban characters.]

ELLEN. Yeah. . . . Everybody's crazy. Everybody's stupid. This is what I think of the world. "And you?" [said Y——]. "Well, sometimes me. But at least I saw it." And then I said, "I don't think I'm a very likable person," and I said that because I know that I was sitting there listening to her listen to me. . . . I heard myself talking. I heard all the things I finally had the nerve to say—which is, "Everybody's crazy." . . . And so finally I just said what I thought about everybody, not caring what anybody thinks, but I listened to myself and said, "Oh . . . this is an unlikable person." . . . Anyway, this guy just says it, and if he says it as a joke, then he doesn't get in trouble for it. . . . These are, I think, really acute perceptions of how ugly things are, and how stupid a lot of things are, and how unreasonable things are.

Later in the interview Ellen developed the point further. Her remarks on Carl and Ramon seemed to me the key to her entire response to Kliban. In Carl's ugliness Kliban was simply recording the ugliness of real people you see. You—and Ellen was talking about herself—want to make up words for that ugliness and tell it to someone. But if you tell it to someone, they will think you a horrible, cruel person. Partly, then, Ellen found ugly people (in or out of cartoons) funny because of her mild frustration, that she could see the ugliness but not tell it.

She also felt distanced. "I'm not like that." But at the same time, underneath, she felt a little frightened that maybe she *was* like that.

This is a cartoon book, however. It proves that someone else sees the world as Ellen sees it. Also it doesn't hurt anybody, although the possibility crossed her mind that Kliban could be sent to prison for portraying this kind of world.

Having said all this once, Ellen went through it a second time by recalling a conversation with a close friend to whom she confided that she saw other people as crazy, stupid, ugly, and unreasonable. But if Kliban says it as a joke, then he doesn't get in trouble for it.

As I understand her, Ellen made three moves in that response. First, she said the Carl and Ramon cartoon depicts something in the real world. It is "out there," as real as people you know who disgust you. Second, she tried to relate to that world by a mutual exchange, but she found the world portrayed by Kliban too ugly and stupid. "I'm not like that." Third, she split her response by creating first a hypothetical, then a real third person: "You want to describe it to someone." She wanted to tell her feelings, but that would take nerve, because it would make her seem not very likable, even horrible, like the Kliban characters. Thus she imagined that this book could send Kliban himself to prison. But the hypothetical third person provided safety, as Kliban does: "Somebody else saw it." And Ellen could exchange her superiority to the Kliban world with someone else who also felt superior. "Nobody's hurt for it." It was just "a jokebook" but also "really acute perceptions." And seeing the ugliness of it all was "a big power trip." Ellen could "see things that other people can't," and she could tell us about them—give to us. Then she would be given to: Y____ would forgive her; her friend at the mixer would rescue her from a "greaser" she didn't want to dance with; or I would assure her that she was smart and clever—as she is.

In effect, Ellen did just what she imagined Kliban doing. He created a real world. She created a real world. He said that world is ugly. So did she. He conveyed this perception to people who admired him for it. So did Ellen. Ellen gave and got just as Kliban gave and got—or, more exactly, as she perceived him giving and getting. Kliban's picture of the world confirmed Ellen's, yes, but more important, it proved you could be safe in holding this view of people, provided you were intelligent and witty enough. Kliban (as Ellen read him) acted out Ellen's own way of coping with her perceptions.

KLIBAN

ELLEN. The captions are ugly, too.

NNH. Yeah. And then there's this mixture of a dark line and a white space.

ELLEN. Yeah, but it comes out of the sense of what you're supposed to do. You're supposed to put in depth, so you can see the depth in the letters. So he does. He makes depth, and it's the ugliest depth, because he can't do it perfectly.

Which is— When I'm thinking about reality— If you can't have perfect people, draw them like they really are. There's something funny about that. . . . In drawing someone this ugly there's an acknowledgment that this is ugliness, and there must be something else that he perhaps can't do. In making the effort to do all this shading, he's acknowledging the fact that there is depth, and that there is a way of drawing depth—

NNH. Right—but he hasn't got it.

ELLEN. He can't—or doesn't. It appears to me that he can't, and what's so funny about it is that he doesn't, that these people are really, really ugly, and you wouldn't expect him to be able to draw someone nice, but they're not just "This is the best I could draw." . . . I think they're probably the best he can draw, but they're not just blah—they're intensely ugly, which makes me think that he has an awareness of what pretty is. And since he can't do it, or doesn't do it, or won't do it, or maybe it isn't funny, he tips it over like the map [a cartoon that is a partially inverted map] and—

Puns are the lowest form of humor, and he does them unabashedly—

NNH. I like that phrase, "He tips it over."

For example, talking about Kliban's style, Ellen singled out his captions. They are ugly, but in a special way. In effect, she says, Kliban acknowledges that there is a right way to draw captions, but he won't (or can't) carry it off. He presents himself as ugly and incapable, just the way he puns unabashedly.

Ellen was stating another way Kliban's style was funny to

her. He acknowledges his own inabilities and imperfections.
Rather than trying to do better (and perhaps failing), he does
his own ugliness or ineptitude intensely. He exaggerates it.
"He tips it over." And Ellen did the same.

She exaggerated her own imperfections, her naiveté about
menstruation, say, or her looking down on poor Carl. Her
jokes often consisted of assigning a nastiness or stupidity to
herself but in an exaggerated, unbelievable form (as in her

Ellen Aging

ELLEN. I'm really concerned about getting old.

NNH. You told me you just had a birthday.

ELLEN. Yeah, but I've always been obsessed with death. Now
I'm obsessed with aging, which means . . . you can chart your
death. I just stare in the mirror, and I find all kinds of lines.
The day I got my job . . . I spent $42 on creams and stuff. The
reason I can't do my thesis is I spend all this time—

NNH. —in front of the mirror—

ELLEN. —rubbing things. I don't even need a mirror anymore.
I know every bump and wrinkle in my face.

"How They Get Fruit"

ELLEN. I really liked it, because I still don't believe that they
pick it off trees. I really have a hard time—

NNH. "How They Get Fruit." I can't remember that one.

ELLEN. Oh, it's people digging it out of a cave. [Actually, out of
the ground.] And my mother used to tell me, these are the
animals you have to know, and these are the fruits, but they
always came in cans, and it never occurred to me that—

NNH. [laughing] . . . they came off trees.

ELLEN. I've never in my life been to an orchard. I mean, I
thought pies grew out of the ground like fruit. I mean I really
did. And . . . the guys mining, digging. I mean fruit is fruit,
and it all comes together, and there's really ugly people
dumping it in baskets, and it's a big factory thing.

overnaive prom poster). She described herself as getting old, although she had just had her twenty-fifth birthday. She said she spent a lot of time buying cosmetics or staring in the mirror at bumps and wrinkles on her face. She used a cartoon captioned "The Nine Warning Signals of Christmas" (showing Santa and eight shapeless reindeer) the same way: to develop her own imperfections. She liked it, she said, "because I love cancer. . . . I think about the nine warning signals all the time. I know them better than the Ten Commandments."

Ellen singled out another cartoon, "How They Get Fruit," to talk about her own ignorance. She grew up, she said, without ever seeing an orchard, so that she thought fruit came only in cans. Naturally, then, she liked Kliban's cartoon showing people mining fruit.

Still another cartoon ("Keeping Bugs Away") showed two frames. In the first ("Bugs"), a desktop with ink, key, book, and pencil holder is covered with horrid scurrying bugs. The second frame ("Bugs Kept Away") shows the same desktop without bugs. Ellen decided it fitted her own experience with desks. She would buy something handsome, but then, once she used it, something would be wrong. Dust, writing on the blotter, something bent, unsharpened pencils would make her desk different from the model desks in Bloomingdale's catalogue.

Responding to "The Nixon Monument," a cartoon showing people staring down into a pit, Ellen said, first, she didn't like it, second, she didn't understand it, and then she gave her interpretation. She thought it showed something phallic missing. "Being a woman I would see that." As the professor who felt responsible for her knowledge of psychoanalysis, I grumbled. In the seminars I teach, I try to get students past automatic symbolism or the theory that woman is a castrated man. But Ellen insisted on casting herself in the role of schematic Freudian. And she did *not* laugh—a point I want to return to.

If you knew Ellen only from this interview, you could get the

Copyright © 1976 B. Kliban. Reprinted from *Never Eat Anything Bigger than Your Head* by permission of Workman Publishing Company, New York.

idea that she was herself snobbish, cruel, vain, and "mundane." Teaching, she looks down on her half-human students. At college she went to the wrong dances and knew grotesque people. If you believed her jokes, you would think this witty, vivacious, attractive young woman an aging hypochondriac who spends all her time fixing her face and worrying about cancer. She eats in contaminated diners. She suffers from penis envy. Her furniture is dirty, and she herself is sloppy. As a psychologist, she is crude, schematic, and old-fashioned. She thinks of herself as an unlikable, "horrible" human being always pointing to the uglinesses and stupidities of others. Yet, in fact, Ellen was one of the most popular and promising people in our graduate program, largely because of these jokes exaggerating her own and others' imperfections.

These were Ellen's informal jokes. In a more formal way, while she was completing her Ph.D., she published a humorous essay modeled loosely on Woody Allen's "Whore of Mensa." The idea is that the graduate student (who is paid by a fellow-

---

"Bugs"

ELLEN. They have pictures of desks and things like that, you know, "How to Arrange Your Study." And I get the same stuff that Bloomingdale's— I bought a teak desk. It was beautiful. Teak Imports in Cambridge. It looks gorgeous. You get it home, and it looks like this [pointing to the first frame]. There's always something wrong with it. There's always dust on it. Or you write on the blotter. Or something bends. Or your pencils aren't sharpened. Or you kill a bug on it—

"The Nixon Monument"

ELLEN. This I don't like. I don't even understand it.

NNH. It's a pit, a slimy pit . . .

ELLEN. Oh, I thought it was . . . phallic, I really did. I thought there was something missing . . .

NNH. All right [laughing]. Someone took it away.

ELLEN. Being a woman I would see that.

NNH. Aw, come on.

ELLEN. No, really. . . . I only know two monuments, the Washington Monument and the Bunker Hill Monument.

NNH. Yeah, and this is the other way.

ELLEN. This is the other way. It looks like the monument fell in, like everybody's looking for something, something of Nixon's.

---

ship for reading books) is a skilled prostitute who gives books incredible pleasures through her sexual devices ("Leather book mark? Yellow highlighter?").

> I seduce the text with a roll of my eyes. Gracefully but firmly, I take it in hand. Slowly, I remove the dust jacket, with full glances at its binding, its corners, and its impressive size. I blow the dust from its belly and lick my fingers longingly as if I'm about to turn the page. "Read me," it cries, "please, oh please read me!"

The story ends when the "I," this combination of graduate student and hooker, is thrown out of the library for trying to read two books at once (one of Ellen's characteristic doublings). The role, again, is not overly flattering—but, because she exaggerated it till it was unbelievable, we gave Ellen the admiration and approving laughter that satisfied her. Her getting us to laugh had created yet another variation on her identity theme, "I give up myself so that a self will give to me." I think her laughing at Kliban did the same.

One could "explain" Ellen's laughter by many of the classic formulas. Clearly she talked about the incongruity Platonists stress, between the high and the low, or as Ellen put it, between the "mundane" and "something really high." She also reported the Aristotelian incongruity between something harmful and its harmless presentation.

She found the cartoons playful. "It's a jokebook. I didn't have to work at it." Although it scarcely seems worth mentioning, the cartoons gave her a sudden sense of fit or resolution.

They embodied archetypal comic rituals, such as killing and eating the hero (King Kong) and scapegoating ("Short on Brains, but a Terrific Dancer"). Like most comedy, they dealt with human beings in society (Norman sucking a toaster?), as opposed to cosmic and tragic figures. Ellen saw the shifts in figure-ground relations (Kliban's harsh blacks and bland whites) with which gestalt psychologists explain laughter. She was also seeing the change of frame around a given statement ("Carl Meets His Match in Ramon") which a follower of Gregory Bateson would note as the playfulness requisite for laughter. And she was perceiving the semioticist's universes of discourse collide (mining fruit; a forest with bear-suited inhabitants).

Ellen enjoyed the way Kliban both makes puns and overmakes them, as if he intended to say both the pun and that he knows better than to pun—an incongruity between is and ought to be. Ellen's amusement answered especially to Hobbes's "sudden glory arising from sudden conception of some eminency in ourselves, by comparison with the infirmity of others." And she was evidently also enjoying Freud's sudden gratification of disguised (or not so disguised) aggressive or sexual impulses.

In short, Ellen's laughing, like most laughings, fits perhaps a dozen new and traditional formulas explaining why we laugh. Paradoxically, if so many formulas apply, no one of them can claim success. Certainly no one theory captures the individuality of Ellen's unique amusement at Kliban's unique cartoons. This curious mingling of success and failure suggests to me the need for some other kind of explanation.

I propose this: Ellen laughs when she recreates her identity. By identity I mean my representation of Ellen's identity theme plus the history of that theme and the variations on it she has lived.

Once I have formulated an identity theme for Ellen, I can use its terms to inquire into her laughing. For example, this was a key passage in Ellen's interview:

> NNH. But why is it funny to take an unpleasant chunk of reality and put it in a cartoon? . . .
> ELLEN. Because it admits that it's there. That's the best part of it, that— You see, I am very critical. . . . And this book proves that somebody else sees what I see.
> NNH. Sees the world as you see it.
> ELLEN. Yeah.

But it isn't quite that Kliban sees the world as Ellen does. I don't know how Kliban sees the world, and neither does Ellen. Kliban *does* let Ellen find *her* view of the world in his cartoons. He draws in such a way that Ellen can see the world as she sees it, but outside herself, in the cartoons. He doesn't "cause" Ellen to laugh. More accurately, he makes it possible for her to achieve laughter in her own individual way.

By proposing an identity theme for Ellen, I make it possible to unfold that process. I can discover a meaning in "somebody else sees what I see." From such themes as "to give and so turn the other from a missed to an imagined to a giving humanity" and "I give of myself so that a self will give to me," I can

ask, "Who are the 'others?'" when Ellen looks at these cartoons? What is being transformed? What self is involved? What
kind of giving is going on? What kind of imagining? What is
"missing"?

There were several "others." Most immediately, there were
the people in the cartoons whom she imagined as realities;
Kliban, as she imagined him; I, as the interviewer and a significant sponsor; a hypothetical third person sympathetic to Ellen's faultfinding; less obviously, Ellen's imagined audience,
either her colleagues, the readers of her own comic writings,
or even you, who have now read about this interview, readers
whom she knew would one day come into being. As the Delphi
group had said two years previously, Ellen tended to think of
all these others as sources from whom she could expect something, and she would get that something by herself giving.

What givings were taking place? Ellen laughed at Kliban and
praised him. She talked gaily and intelligently to me. She would
joke herself, for my benefit, yours, and anyone else's. She
acted naive. She played the subordinate student, even school-
girl. She agreed to be tape recorded and transcribed. Most important, she agreed to think about and associate to her laughter.

She gave of herself, that is, her wit and personality. By giving, she doubled. She said Kliban was doing what she would
do, for example, by finding allusions in the cartoons (as her
own comic essay alludes to Woody Allen's). She structured the
cartoons into twos: right-wrong, black-white, don't-do-this-do-
that. She tried to obey these instructions and do what Kliban
seemingly expected of her—but she laughed at the silliness of
doing so, thus giving to him both ways. She transformed us
others from missing persons to people imagined as there but
not yet satisfactory sources: Kliban as half-incompetent artist;
me as an expert, but one she could quibble with; all the characters and settings of the cartoons as gross, "mundane" reality;
and finally herself as stupid, ugly, inept, and base.

This last move was a key one. By inventing failings for herself, she would be forgiven for pointing to the failings of others.

By giving the benefit of the doubt to Kliban (he's not really so inept), she would be given the benefit of the doubt herself. Indeed, she could become superior. By imagining the rest of the world as low, she could become high. By giving wit, she would be given wit; that is, she would be seen as witty—for (to return to the theme I see underlying all her remarks) to give to an other turns that other from an absent or (basely) imagined to a giving humanity.

Understanding Ellen's amusement as a function of her identity, we can at last answer the question with which this case study opened. Why did Ellen laugh at the King Kong cartoon? Because it presents and suddenly resolves an incongruity between the high and the low. Because it presents something harmful (King Kong) harmlessly. Because it is playful. Because it shows people eating the slain god. Because it let her gratify her aggressive impulses toward those little people in the diner and the giant Kong. Because it let her feel superior to both of them. All of the above.

But she would *not* have laughed had this cartoon not shown an other, a "real" other, the diner, "there." Moreover, she could imagine the other really giving (food) to her precisely because she both gave up self and made the diner real by making herself part of the grubbiness of the scene: "That was so perfect—because I've eaten there." She could put her identity into playful question (How am I related to this cartoon?) but resolve her own question in a personally satisfying way. I lower myself by putting myself into the grubbiness of this cartoon, but then it gives me two things: a sudden, playful answer to its riddle and—something personally important to me—food.

Ellen thus made it possible to say both why she in particular laughed at Kliban's cartoons and why we in general all laugh at the pieces of reality we call funny: *because we recreate our identities by means of a stimulus.*

But what does that mean? Since (by definition) we are all confirming and recreating our identities all the time, what's special about laughing? Since Ellen's identity differs from every other human being's, how can it explain anything about your or my laughing? What's the relation between the incongruities and rituals and aggression and superiority we all experience and the identity that is Ellen's alone? Identity may explain what's funny, but it's a funny sort of explanation.

11 *Why the Rest of Us Laugh*

Ellen laughed because she found she could confirm her identity through Kliban's cartoons. That is the general principle I get from our case study. "This book proves that somebody else sees what I see."

This theory, however, opens up questions besides why we laugh. I see three big ones. How do we extend that highly individual explanation of Ellen's laughing to someone else? How does this identity explanation fit into the two hundred or so traditional theories I so laboriously surveyed? (Did I waste my time and yours?) And the knottiest of all: Isn't my reading of Ellen's laughing and her identity a function of *my* identity as well as hers?

Our case study may explain why Ellen laughs. Can it explain why anybody else laughs? Shouldn't I have looked at a larger sample (as I did in *5 Readers Reading*)?

As it happens, we have a second laugher conveniently nearby—me. Why did I find the Nixon Monument cartoon so funny? I saw it differently from Ellen, as "a pit, a slimy pit."

ELLEN. I thought there was something missing.
NNH: It reminds me of that famous Herblock cartoon where Nixon is climbing up out of a sewer waving a brush, and he's got this five-o'clock shadow that he always had, and Nixon wrote in and complained to Herblock, "Would you want your children to see you in a picture like this?" So he [Herblock] redrew it and took off the five-o'clock shadow.

I laughed by making Nixon into a father who had tried to smear others and ended up smearing himself. He had gone down and into a dirty place and been dirtied by it. By seeing him that way I attacked an authority who was "in" in several senses. The cartoon enabled me to assert such a father's private dirt against his public professions of probity.

According to Freud's theory of jokes, I gratified an aggressive wish. True. That wish is (according to the identity theory of jokes) a function of my identity but not necessarily others' and certainly not Ellen's.

As I read myself, my identity includes such themes as fathers, private and public, and inside and outside. I know they have played a painfully important part in my emotional life, going back to early childhood. I know they inform my personal loathing of Richard Nixon and my malicious laughter at this cartoon. I am laughing because I confirm my identity through something outside myself.

I laugh, in other words, for exactly the same reason Ellen did, and further, I think I could demonstrate over and over again that anybody who finds this cartoon funny is also thereby confirming identity.

In claiming that, however, I am generalizing differently from the usual interpretations of laughter, which explain it in terms of incongruity or superiority or arousal. Incongruity applies the same way to all cartoons. Superiority or arousal apply the same way to all laughers. The idea of confirming identity applies to all laughers at all cartoons, *but* in a different way for each. Ellen and I did, each of us, confirm our identities through Kliban, but my identity was different from hers.

In other words, as some experimentalists have begun to ask, is there any such thing as a joke? "Nothing is funny to everyone and anything seems potentially funny to someone." Hence, they conclude, "a 'joke,' defined as a humorous stimulus (external to the observer), non-exists."[1] Or, you could say, amusement, like beauty, is in the eye of the beholder. Perhaps the odd kind of generalization yielded by identity theory can give us a way of bridging the gap between such universal principles as incongruity and superiority and the uniqueness of your sense of humor or mine.

There is yet another problem, however, with this large principle. I defined identity (above, pp. 129–30) as a continuing attempt to put into words a pattern that is revealed in *everything* a person does. If Ellen confirms her identity in everything she does, then she confirms it in the cartoons she doesn't laugh at as well as the ones she does.

Although she did not laugh at "The Nixon Monument," she used the cartoon characteristically, to deplete herself. "Being a woman, I would see" it as a joke on "something [phallic] missing." But "I don't even understand it." Slow puzzling countered sudden laughter. More important, "something missing" did not suit Ellen's identity. She wanted to transform a "something missing" into a "something there" that would give. "Everybody's looking for something, something of Nixon's." Similarly, a definition of woman as castrate (again, "something missing") was not an idea this feminist could be playful about. We do not laugh when we feel our identity in jeopardy.

Ellen did not laugh at "The Nixon Monument" because she did not find it playful and she did not find it sudden. Paradoxically, then, the "conditions" theories, seemingly so obvious and so widely and tacitly accepted as scarcely to be worth mentioning, turn out to be decisive. They enable us to set laughter apart from other identity-confirming human activities. It is not enough to say we laugh when we confirm our identities through a stimulus outside ourselves. Rather, *we laugh when we have recreated our identities through a stimulus suddenly and playfully* ("suddenly" and "playfully" themselves being relative to identity).

But even as I suggest (or proclaim?) this principle, I wonder why the almost trivially obvious conditions that theorists scarcely trouble to mention turn out to be the important theories. What about incongruity and superiority and relief and arousal and myth and liberation and all the rest?

When Schopenhauer concluded that we laugh at the angle between a circle and its tangent, he may not have been speaking for you and me, but he must have spoken, if we credit him with any honesty at all, for himself. He must have meant at the very least that *he* laughed. So, too, must Aristotle and Bergson and Pascal and Hobbes and all the rest.

Each of these theories says something at least about one person—its inventor. Each must therefore describe some sort of automatic or intermediate action in one person's laughing. If one person, perhaps another, and perhaps another after that. Indeed, a great many people *might* make use of an incongruity between what is and what ought to be or a sense of sudden glory in order to laugh. But I don't see that any one of these theories describes a *necessary* condition for your or my laughing.

To be sure, laughing does feel as though something mental triggered a quite automatic physical process, as though we were explosive mechanisms and something like a sense of sudden glory set us off. "We do not laugh, but 'something laughs in us,'" as our semioticist said.

If, however, the mental trigger posited by Hobbes or Freud or Aristotle were all it took to make someone laugh, then we could predict laughter with certainty. But we can't. Nobody "makes" anybody laugh (except by tickling or laughing gas). A whim, one's *amour propre*, a painful association, some distracting memory—within the total transaction almost any passing mood can counteract a sense of sudden glory, the gratification of a sexual impulse, or the perception of an incongruity.

None of these things necessarily leads to laughter. Even so, when Ellen laughed at Kliban, I thought I could trace half a dozen of these theories in the cartoons or in her remarks about them. The theories seem likely, informative, "there" in any given laughing, yet ultimately they don't explain what they set out to explain. How shall we understand this halfway validity?

Genetically, laughing is something all humans do more or less the same way, like walking upright or sneezing or speaking. We share our social as well as our biological heritage when we laugh, although we laugh at different things and in different ways. Similarly, you and I both speak English, although we speak with different tones and vocabularies—in short, with different styles. Because we have *styles* of walking, speaking, sneezing, and laughing, I conclude that they all take place within a larger transaction of identity.

That "within" is only one of many metaphors we have for this kind of partial likeness. We say that the individual and his culture or biology "combine" or "add" as if the relation were arithmetic. Or we speak of social or biological "factors" (multiplication). We often talk in terms of social "forces" or the "impact" of a biological event or the "pressure" of the group on the individual, as though the relation were one of mechanics, as in freshman physics. I say, for example, that I am "moved" by a tragedy. Sometimes we say that society or biology "forms" or "molds" or "shapes" us, as if the individual were the artist's clay (but who is the artist, then?). Or we speak, as I just did, of our social and biological "heritage," as of a piece of property one could inherit. We say that culture is "one element" in laughing, as if we were talking about a chemical reaction or a machine with many parts. And my own word "within" could mean something spatial or one process governed by a larger process.[2]

I don't think these metaphors are "wrong," but I believe we can find a more precise way to represent a process that is the same but different for all of us, as laughing is. I am thinking of one of the great discoveries of the twentieth century. We humanists have not used it for thinking about humans as much perhaps as we should: feedback systems.

If I see the highway ahead of me turn right, I turn the steering wheel of my car right. I do so in such a way that I can see the car's right front fender remain at the same distance from the right side of the road that it has been. If I see the right fender get too close to the shoulder, I turn the steering wheel left. In other words, my behavior with the wheel controls my perception of the distance between the right side of the car and the edge of the highway. As the title of a very useful book by a computer scientist in this field suggests, behavior is the control of perception.[3]

Interestingly, that is exactly the way Freud defines a wish in the last, metapsychological chapter of *The Interpretation of Dreams*. A wish seeks to recreate the perception of a satisfaction.[4] According to the "pleasure principle," all our waking behavior serves to gratify a wish—as opposed to our dreams, in which we merely hallucinate our pleasures. Either way, however, a wish is a wish for a certain perception, and thus, for Freud, as for the computer scientist, the aim of behavior is the control of perception.

Before attempting a verbal metaphor, let me provide a diagram of a feedback loop (see Figure 1). A feedback loop has to have three things. First, a behavioral end that acts on the input—my hands turning the steering wheel. Second, a comparator, such as my eyes and brain figuring out the distance between the right wheel and the shoulder. That comparison, my seeing, becomes the perceptual end that the behavioral end controls. Third, and this is the crucial item that is often left out, some standard or reference signal that is outside and unaf-

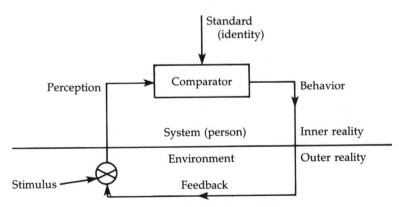

FIGURE 1. A one-loop feedback model for a person

fected by that loop in which behavior controls perception—such as my need to keep three feet from the edge of the road.

Although some psychology textbooks treat feedback loops as though they were self-contained, there has to be that reference level from outside. Somebody has to set the thermostat. If I had an autopilot for my car, it could keep the right wheels a fixed distance from the edge of the road, but I would have to tell it what that fixed distance should be. And it is the independence of that outside reference or standard that lets me use feedback as a metaphor for Ellen's laughing.

When I lecture on Kliban's cartoons and the slide of "The Nixon Monument" comes on, I always hear a big laugh. That physical cachinnation is the part of laughing all of us do alike, and evidently many people in 1980s America feel amused at that particular gibe at Richard Nixon. But then there is the part of laughing that is completely individual, that led me to find "The Nixon Monument" a funny smear and Ellen to remain hesitant and unmoved at "something missing."

I was able to confirm my identity through that cartoon, and Ellen was not. We could image our different responses by the feedback diagram. Ellen "set," as it were, the standard for her laughing in terms of her identity: giving in order to be given to. She was not able to see the cartoon in such a way that it fitted her standard. I set the standard in terms of a dirty father, and I did get positive feedback.

In other words, we can imagine humor in two parts. The first part, a standard, comes from the individual's identity and governs the other part: a loop in which the individual engages the cartoon so as to get a perception that satisfies the standard. Identity talks about the first part. The theorists of humor (with such rare exceptions as those who administer the Mirth Response Test) talk only about the second part.

Notice that we can describe that first part quite precisely, as when I and the rest of the Delphi seminar addressed Ellen's identity. To be sure, we used words rather than numbers, but language has its precisions too. How directly does a given theme interrelate the person's actions? How many actions does it deal with? Like Sherlock Holmes, we provided stronger and weaker analyses.

One reads identity as it acts through behavior and perception. One could hardly do otherwise. Similarly, it would be difficult, perhaps impossible, to analyze the second part, the loop in which behavior controls perception, without understanding it in relation to identity. That would be like trying to understand the movements of the car without knowing that somebody was trying to keep it three feet from the right edge of a road. Or like trying to understand the "behavior" of a television set by studying its wiring and knobs and what it emitted, while "controlling for"—blocking out of the analysis— the person choosing the channels. Yet that is what many theorists of the comic seem to be trying to do. I think that is why their theories have a kind of halfway validity.

What we have learned from Ellen is that we can fit her to a great many theories, Hobbes and Aristotle no less than Freud and Lichtenstein. To be valid, however, the theories have to fit her, not vice versa. Hobbes has to open up Ellen's singular sense of superiority. Aristotle has to account for her unique rejections of the ugly. The incongruists need to reveal Ellen's special sense of what is high and low or ideal and real. Freud and psychoanalysis have to unfold Ellen's particular kind of sexual or aggressive satisfaction. An explanation of humor must admit the various incongruities and superiorities and reassurances that our theorists have come up with, but Ellenize them.

Arousal and superiority and relief and incongruity are probably "there" in some sense in that lower loop, the feedback controlling perception. We need, though, to look at the reference levels responsive to identity to understand what arousal and superiority and relief and incongruity are doing. That would be understanding the "behavior" of the car or television set by taking into account the person turning the steering wheel or the tuning knob. Then the wiring and the knobs and the programs can all make sense together. If we take into account the identities of the laughers, the two hundred theories and variations of theories can then explain the comic and laughing and laughings.

There are two directions—at least two—along which I can explore the way Ellen or I find something funny, or, indeed, the way anyone transacts any chunk of reality. In one, I can ask how we allow Kliban's blacks and whites to enter our minds and how we allow the inner world of our private beliefs about Nixon to permeate Kliban's blacks and whites. This is an axis between self and other. The other direction has to do with time. When Ellen says the cartoon shows something phallic missing, she is setting this new stimulus in the context of her whole life as a woman in a patriarchal society. When I imagine Nixon as a father, I am interpreting the cartoon in relation to my own long relationship with my father. In other words, Ellen and I are setting the cartoon in immediate time, the now of our expectations and gratifications, but we are also giving it a meaning beyond immediacy.

These are two—what shall I say?—metaphysical axes along which we transact reality: time and space. We can understand these two axes in psychological terms as well as philosophically, however. For example, I can understand the inner-outer of Ellen's laughing at Kliban's cartoons through the familiar psychoanalytic terms fantasy and defense. Defense: what does she admit in from the not-self and how does she shape it in order to admit it? Fantasy: what clusters of wishes and fears does she project from the inner world of self onto the outer worlds of the cartoons?

Along the boundary between long time and short, she mingles expectation and transformation. By "expectation" I mean the particular mixture of trust and mistrust she brings to another. More specifically, how does she fit these particular cartoons into the here-and-now sequence of her wishes about this and other experiences? When I say "transformation," I can ask the opposite: How does she give these cartoons a meaning or value beyond the immediate here and now?

In the interview Ellen made these different modes or DEFTings fairly explicit. (Defense, expectation, fantasy, and transformation lead to a convenient acronym: DEFT.) For example, expectation: "I don't have to talk about it. They're pictures. . . . It's just like watching TV—you don't have to do anything. And it's not like me telling a joke." Ellen expected the cartoons to give her relief from her normal alertness and joking.

Defense: Kliban permits Ellen to be "overly critical" of people. "It admits that it's there." That is, the cartoon book portrays an ugly part of reality. "This guy just says it [what I think about everybody], and if he says it as a joke, then he doesn't get in trouble for it. These are, I think, really acute perceptions of how ugly things are."

Ellen found more personal defenses, however, in Kliban's work. She created from these cartoons a horrid—and, she would insist, realistic—picture of herself in association with gross, vulgar, stupid dances, schools, restaurants, magazines, furniture, and relationships. She was helplessly subject to these vulgarities, until she brought her wit and intelligence into play and reasserted control. "I'm not like that. See, I can think of all the words that describe it, and I'm not that."

So Ellen doubled herself: she became both "in" and not "in" the cartoons, both "above" them and "beneath" them—in two places at once. In the incongruities between high and low, raunchy and not raunchy, in the right-wrong and don't-do-that-do-this cartoons, she found a duality that fitted her defenses and adaptations toward the world. By giving—submitting—herself to the cartoons, by making them real, she made them give her satisfaction. She became both donor and donee.

The fantasies (that is, the clusters of wishes and fears) she projected onto the cartoons took a matching form. On the one hand she imagined herself stuck in Kliban's gross and grubby world. On the other she imagined herself superior to all that, because she knew and understood it.

Here, as in life generally, fantasy and defense closely resemble each other, since our defensive and adaptive strategies must gratify needs and give pleasure as well as ward off anxiety. Otherwise we would find other defenses and adaptations that do. Here Ellen (as I interpret what she said) gratified her wishes to be superior but also to submit. She shaped the cartoons to admit these conflicting wishes by, so to speak, dualizing them. She saw Kliban as both unconsciously and consciously crude: "He does them unabashedly." She saw herself as implicated in the crudity the cartoons portray but also outside and superior to it.

To the extent that she made the cartoons mean anything in the long term, she carried over this dualistic giving and being given to into such "themes" as the allusions she found to *Oliver Twist* and Woody Allen. When she endowed the cartoons with these allusions, the cartoons showed her own sophistication.

Her association to eavesdropping on her parents as they talked over a school visit suggests a larger theme, however. "Do they know I'm listening?" "Am I dreaming this?" Ellen made Kliban's world real. "I've had students like this." But behind the belief that Kliban is giving "acute perceptions of how ugly things are" lie deeper questions: Is reality really like this? Am I? What is real? What can I believe in?

By exploring defenses, expectations, fantasies, and transformations in Ellen's remarks about Kliban, I can trace here and there the way Ellen is acting out some of the general theories of laughter: Hobbes's superiority or Platonic incongruity or Aristotle's harmless ugliness. I also, however, find Ellen living out a general principle that applies to any laugher. She—and the rest of us—laugh because we suddenly, playfully confirm our identities through something outside ourselves. She DEFTS Kliban's cartoons.

But we are always confirming our identities through something outside ourselves—that is the definition of identity. In transacting a joke, a person brings to bear the same DEFT as for any other separate being or event. I should be able, then, to draw some connections between the traditional theories of the comic and DEFT. DEFT should provide a way to link incongruity and the rest to other, clinical or perceptual psychologies.

Notice, first, that we see a joke or a cartoon in two modes. It develops a particular story about tilting with windmills or eating King Kongburgers. Its particular story aside, however, a joke or a cartoon is simply an other, and one responds to it as to any others, be they persons, things, or texts.

Considering the joke both as other and as story, I can trace some shadowy parallels between the four terms of DEFT and the four nonphysiological concerns of our theorists (see Table 2). The closest match comes between psychological defenses

TABLE 2. Rough correspondences between
DEFT and theories of laughter

Joke as other and as story	Comic theory
Expectation	Stimulus
Defense	Conditions
Fantasy	Psychology
Transformation	Catharsis

and the conditions for the comic (suddenness and the play frame). A laugher uses the play frame—no one was really hurt in that pratfall—to get rid of any threat to himself from the joke as other. Laughers also use the suddenness of the funny as a defense. Quick relief allays anxiety.

A laughing audience gives rise to a particularly powerful defense, for the laughter of others (as our ethologists have told us) reassures the human animal. The sound of others' laughing says there *is* a frame. Conversely, I feel particularly defensive and worried when I watch some hapless comic trying to amuse a "cold" nightclub audience and failing.

Timing and playfulness depend not only on the comic situation (a nightclub, a cartoon book) but also on the form and content of the particular joke. "Take my wife—Please!" As in that brilliantly brief one-liner of Henny Youngman's (which for a time became a "Jonestown one-liner": "Take my life— Please!"), a joke can end so quickly that we have no time to mobilize anxiety, no time, really, to do anything but get set for a joke. Alternatively, a long story (such as the five-minute anecdotes of Ronnie Corbett) can amuse us provided it is surrounded with a play frame, like a shaggy-dog story. Timing itself can be the content of a joke, as in the Polish joke about Polish jokes. "Ask me what's wrong with most Polish jokes," says the teller. "OK, what's wrong with—" "Timing!" he bursts in.

Timing depends very much on the way we fit it to the particular content of the particular joke, but the play frame pervades all forms of the comic, particularly as part of our expectation. Some jokes let us know they are jokes right away. The white space and caption of a cartoon or a phrase such as "traveling salesman" or "desert island" or "There were a minister, a priest, and a rabbi . . ." provide the conventional shield of a play frame (as the anthropologists point out).

Professional comics know that such obvious lead-ins as "Have you heard the one about . . . ?" kill the joke. The hearer tenses: Will I find this funny? To avoid that reaction, the professionals leave the truth or falsity of what they are about to say ambiguous: "A funny thing happened to me on the way to the studio" or "The hotel room they gave me is so small the mice have to take turns inhaling."

We get ready to play when we hear an obvious comic frame. At a statement that may or may not be a joke, we tense, but then the suddenness with which we can put the play frame into reassuring effect becomes an even richer basis for laughter. But if someone is asking, Do you find this funny? Will you laugh?, you don't, and that is why books about laughter can be so deadly.

In other words, expectation (in the DEFT transaction) can take in the joke as definitely that—a joke—or as something quite ambiguous. Either way, however, we EXPECT gratification from our DEFTing.

The jokester is telling us this for some reason, presumably to please us. Out of cognitive, ethical, or formal incongruity we can create a "strained expectation" that then (in Kant's theory) bursts like a bubble. One may also expect the comic catharsis or simply a sudden burst of pleasure in laughter. In other words, what we expect from jokes generally, as other, as not-self, depends a great deal on our past experience with jokes. Then the particular words of this joke let us expect this or that particular, as in Berlyne's "collative" properties.

The DEFT model, however, cues me to look for a general expectation of pleasure from the "joke as other" and also for some particular expectation, the gratification of some particular wish or cluster of wishes—fantasy. Fantasy in DEFTing corresponds to what the psychologists of laughter talked about: relief (Dewey), hostility and superiority (Hobbes), unconscious sex and aggression (Freud), or the various traits experimentalists have tested. Within a DEFTing, these qualities correspond to various fantasies projected onto the joke as an other. Some are just about universal (the desire to feel superior). Others are quite particular to an individual (such as rejecting religion in the Mirth Response Test).

A particular story lets me project my particular wishes into it, that the traveling salesman seduce the farmer's daughter or King Kong be turned into little hamburgers. At the same time, however, the particular joke may be open to well-nigh universal fantasies, the archetypes and stock characters of the human comedy. Thus the *eiron* and *alazon* of prehistoric Attic comedy turn up in Broadway musicals as each new generation rediscovers them in their lives.

As I project my particular and shared fantasies onto the joke, I expect (or trust) they will be jokingly managed. I trust I will gratify my fantasies within the security of play, and laugh. To the extent I trust that I will find laughter and gratification within a play frame, I have defended against anything I find threatening in the joke. Then the joke by its particular mimetic form may enable me to make that pleasure sudden, hence more casual, more playful, but more defended against, and therefore easier. Then, having laughed, I will feel the satisfaction I was looking for in the first place.

The last term, the T of DEFT, refers to that satisfaction. To laugh I must feel a "point"—a transformation, therefore. I give the sexual, aggressive, or other fantasies I projected onto the comic text some moral, social, aesthetic, or intellectual focus. This is the "point" with which comic catharsis begins, the feeling that my laughter makes a satisfying sense.

Defense (out of the four terms of the DEFT model) corresponds fairly closely to theories about the conditions for laughter and the comic. Fantasy names what the psychologists of laughter consider. Ideas of comic catharsis fit the DEFT model of transformation. The most ambiguous of the four terms, however, is expectation.

At the most basic level, I expect a joke or a comedy to please me as jokes and comedies have done before. I expect the DFT of DEFT. For example, I expect to gratify a satisfyingly hostile, sexual, or selfish fantasy suddenly, playfully, and with a justifying "point." In any laughing, it is the sudden gratification of all the components (D's, F's, and T's) of my original expectation that constitutes the confirmation of me that will issue in laughter.

We could put all these correspondences between DEFT and the laughing relationship into a table (see Table 3). We can also understand different genres of the comic from the various DEFT terms. For example, as Freud pointed out, gratifying a taboo wish (fantasy) is simply uncomfortable. Gratifying an allowed wish yields a frothy sort of fun—the jest. Gratifying a tabooed wish which is defended against and given a point—that is the joke. Defense and transformation, then, mark off the simpler jest from the true joke or the *Don Quixote* made out of many jokes.

Different defenses match the several types of the comic, as Freud defined them. If an other is victimized but cannot retaliate, we have the joke with its tendentious "point." Nonsense

TABLE 3. Correspondences between DEFT and theories of humor

Joke as other (any joke)	Joke as story (this particular joke)
Expectation	
Of DFT	Of DFT
Ambiguous (incongruity)	From start of joke
Defense	
A condition	A condition
Play frame (e.g.,	Timing
an audience)	
Fantasy	
Projection and gratification	Projection and gratification of
of personal impulses toward	particular wishes admitted by
sex, superiority, hostility,	this joke
or relief	Archetypal elements
Transformation	
Catharsis	A "point": the resolution or
Social	acceptance of a particular
Transcendent	incongruity
Expectations of DFT satisfied	Expectations of DFT satisfied

or the jest combine nontendentious fun with ego defenses (such as splitting, omitting, or displacing attention to language). We get something like the nonsense limericks of Edward Lear or Lewis Carroll's "Hunting of the Snark." If the other is perceived as unharmed and harmless, we have the comic. If the other is forgiving, we have humor based on superego defenses (denial or projection of guilt): Dickens or E. B. White.

None of these jokes or genres exists in the abstract, however, because jokes do not have fantasies or defenses—people do. Only when some person laughs has the joke become a psychological event. And only when many people laugh does it become a social one. But that is the normal situation for jokes, many people laughing.

. So far, I have used the combination of identity and feedback to accent the individual in Ellen's or my laughing. There was, obviously, a strong social element as well. Ellen's laughter licensed mine, as mine did hers. As Freud pointed out, the joke (but not the comic or humor) serves the benign but paradoxical social function of asserting our shared inhibitions by the very act of loosening them. By laughing together, Ellen and I let each other know that we held certain values in common.

Social groups were, I take it, what Freud had in mind when he commented (as Lorenz many years later would do): "Every joke calls for a public of its own and laughing at the same jokes is evidence of far-reaching psychical conformity." Freud observed that "among country people or in inns of the humbler sort" smutty jokes start up when the barmaid or the innkeeper's wife appears. He concluded they thus reveal their theme—exposure. In these rough-hewn settings the mere "uttering of an undisguised indecency" raises a laugh. In "a society of more refined education," the joke has to take on more of a formal disguise. "The greater the discrepancy between what is given directly in the form of smut and what it . . . calls up in the hearer, the more refined becomes the joke and the higher, too, it may venture to climb into good society."[5]

Evidently social and economic class, degree of urbanity or rusticity, and level of education all provide schemata with which we are amused or not. Nationality must be another source. The oddity of "the English sense of humor" is proverbial, but the French, the Japanese, or the American must seem just as strange to someone from another culture, and all must seem equally odd to *Star Trek*'s Mr. Spock, who never laughs at all.

Perhaps the best way of thinking about these national senses of humor is as the laughter of a macroperson.[6] To arrive at an "American sense of humor," one could begin extensionally, including and excluding things according to whether you would agree or not with the statement "Americans find this funny." Then think of all the included things as the amusements of one huge person, and formulate an identity theme for that composite person. (I imagine such a macroperson by recalling the often reproduced frontispiece of Hobbes's *Leviathan*, showing a giant figure of the state composed of dozens of little figures of individual human beings.) If we can understand one person's sense of humor as a function of that person's identity, we may be able to explore the "American" or the "French" or the "Southern" sense of humor in terms of a macroperson's identity.

Other groups besides nations play a part, too. I am a college professor. I don't mind jokes that suggest that professors are eccentric or absent-minded (I am), but I don't enjoy jokes that suggest we are impractical (I am not!) or that what we have to teach is not worth learning. Shaw said, "He who can, does. He who cannot, teaches," and I am not amused. I prefer "He who can, does. He who knows better, teaches."

Culture goes even deeper, however, permeating the very perceptions on which laughter must be based. You and I, for example, live amid straight lines and right angles and corners in what anthropologists call a "carpentered" world. Zambians do not. Where we can see a certain picture made up of straight lines as a box shown in perspective, they see only a flat, two-dimensional design.[7]

Colin Turnbull reports that his BaMbuti guide, who lived in a forest where the greatest distance he could see was a hundred feet, could not recognize buffalo grazing some miles away as buffalo. He called them insects and even tried to identify the species. When Turnbull and the guide drove closer and found that the insects were indeed buffalo, the guide explained the change by saying that he had been deluded by witchcraft when they had been at a distance.[8]

In effect, the guide demonstrated two things. First, culture can limit biology, removing some possibilities in even so basic a visual schema as the correlation of size and distance.[9] Second, if so, culture must even more deeply and pervasively color the way we perceive family relations, politics, the meanings of words, and what we find funny.

In our feedback metaphor, we can take the role of culture into account by resorting to a two-tier diagram (see Figure 2). As before, the human being lives in the world by means of behavior that controls perception. That is the lower loop: a person acts on the physical world to change perceptions for the better. An upper loop lets me visualize the way a "social factor" such as language can limit or add to biology.

That is, I have a tongue and vocal cords with which to speak, ears with which to hear, and (so Noam Chomsky might say) part of my brain wired for language. In that sense, my body, like every other normal human being's, is equipped for language. But I speak English and not Italian. That means I can't even hear the difference between "rr" and "r" in Italian, and even though I speak some French, I have trouble not hearing "nom" and "non" differently.

In other words, my culture alters what my physiology can hear. For example, my culture equips my body with a language. So provided, I can fashion the thoughts you are reading. But that language also puts limits to what I can hear or think.

Further, my English is not quite the same as yours. I speak with a certain drawl and pitch. When I write I use such words as "nevertheless" and "however" more than most people do. In linguistic jargon, I write and speak an idiolect *and* a dialect *and* a language. My identity sets the standards for my particular brand of English, which in turn tunes my body's speech equipment to certain sounds and not to others.

Language, tools, cooking, family structure all provide standards for eyes, ears, legs, and fingers. The ground of our lives is physical and biological, yet culture can limit our biology, as with the BaMbuti guide.

Figure 2 provides a metaphor for him. Quite unconsciously, you or I would "set" our reference levels for judging distances. We would program ourselves with data about the angles, the hues, or the sizes and sounds that indicate a buffalo is two miles away. We do so by means of cultural resources, but the BaMbuti's culture has never let him learn about a buffalo two miles away. In effect the social loop has not set a reference level for the biophysical loop, and a buffalo two miles away simply can't exist for him.

Yet culture can also enlarge biology. The BaMbuti has skills in tracking and hunting I cannot even imagine. In my own culture a hammer lets me drive nails that I could not drive with my bare hands. Finally the individual *uses* the hammer or *works with* his inability to see buffalo at a distance (says it is witchcraft).

As Erikson said, there is no person without society. Identities, even in this theme-and-variations sense, are social and political as well as individual. More precisely, identities are the way people are social and political. Still more precisely, identities are a way to describe the way people are social and political.

Culture does not pressure so much as it either confines or broadens us. To be sure, society may make one or another choice very costly, but society cannot physically coerce as chains or drugs do. It is not accurate to say that Serge or Sophie laughs at a certain joke "because" he is male or she is female, an American, a graduate student, or a temporary resident of Buffalo. Serge and Sophie bring these and many other things from their biological and cultural heritage to bear on Kliban's cartoons in their characteristic ways, that is, as transactions of their identities.

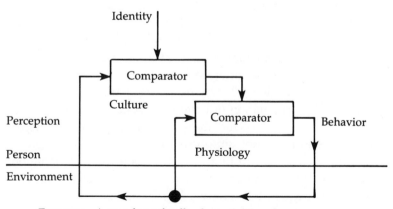

FIGURE 2. A two-loop feedback model for a person

In those transactions, culture defines some things as possible and others as not possible for an individual to choose. It is possible for a culture to deny some individuals some choices (to see buffalo at two miles), but that is the only way culture physically "coerces."

In our feedback metaphor, the individual sets the limits within which culture sets the limits within which he physiologically acts on the world so as to control his perceptions. To be sure, physical and social realities tend to be more stable than the individual, but the individual uses that stability to satisfy his own constantly changing desires. Metaphors of social "forces" or "determinism" do not quite convey that curious mixture of limitation and freedom.

I think it more accurate to say that the individual uses (or is limited by) cultural resources that in turn use (or are limited by) human biology and physical realities. By the combination of using and being limited by, I intend a relation like that in the two-loop feedback model. If I hammer a nail or turn a phrase, I use and am limited by the tool and the language.

With such a feedback metaphor, we can think through the trickiest paradox of all, that this explanation is *my* explanation. Explanations span the whole hierarchy of feedback networks. At the physical level, they enable us to make sense of the stable world we perceive and to live successfully in it. At the cultural level, we accept only certain kinds of things as explanations. No leprechauns. Stability. But finally, at a personal level, this is *my* explanation, arrived at *my* way, stated in *my* style. And that can be different from yours.

Why does Ellen laugh? Why do I laugh? Why do the rest of us laugh? An explanation of laughter through identity asks for action by the explain*er* and the explain*ed-to* as well as the explain*ed*. Identity is not simply a category like "incongruity" which is filled or not to fit an "if this, then that" explanation, such as "If there is a sudden incongruity, people will laugh." Rather, a statement of identity calls for feedback. It is a way of asking, Can I understand Ellen's actions as a unity? Can you understand them so? Can we compare our understandings? Neither she nor I nor you passively experience jokes—or explanations—the way billiard balls obediently carom and click to Newton's laws. Or the way people once thought billiard balls obeyed laws.

An older idea of discovery modeled itself on exploration or history. The nineteenth-century historian believed his job was to find out and describe "what really happened." Scientists found laws that were just "there" waiting to be discovered, like Antarctica.

Today most of us believe that scientists not only discover the world but shape it by the very act of discovering it. Scientists do not simply find "what is there," because the methods and assumptions they bring determine what they can find. They discover a mixture: the world, but also how to make sense of the world and bring it into the feedbacks by means of which they know our world and act on it. Science is not just a textbookful of principles, a product, but the process that yielded that product.

To put it another way, science itself fits Figure 2, our metaphorical diagram combining stable process and stable but mercurial individual. Science as stable process uses the lowest feedback loop: testing physical reality. But the scientific culture determines what physical tests qualify as "scientific." In the stable middle loop, the scientific community defines the methods and assumptions of science, the culture of science both limiting and enlarging the physical realities scientists deal with.[10] Finally, at the top level, some particular scientist uses the methods and assumptions of science, and changes them, if necessary, as reality responds this way or that, as we pass from a period of "normal science" to one of scientific "revolution."

We can use the feedback metaphor to ask: What is the relation of an explanation through identity to more familiar scientific explanations of, say, the carom and click of billiard balls? Can an identity explanation be "valid" or "scientific" at all?

After all, identity is something *I* infer, and my inference is surely a function of *my* identity as well as of a communal technique of interpreting events as a theme and variations. As in the Delphi seminar, different people saw Ellen's identity differently—as functions of *their* identities—although they used similar thought processes. When I say Ellen laughs as she suddenly, playfully reaffirms her wish to be given to by a real other, *her* identity includes both *my* skill and *my* character. I am skilled at discovering themes (as literary critics are). Characteristically, I intellectualize, I visualize, I see things in pairs, and I translate human actions into inanimate mechanisms (such as feedback systems).

I cannot claim, then, that I have reached back into the past and explained in some absolute way why Ellen laughed when she first saw these cartoons. Maybe she was at a picnic or a party, tipsy or high, when first she laughed at *Never Eat Anything Bigger than Your Head*. For that reason, if for no other, I cannot recreate the spark of amusement that led to her laughing last year, the day before, or even twenty seconds previously, but that is not what Ellen and I were trying to do.

Sitting on my living-room floor with the tape recorder between us, Ellen and I created a "potential space" into which she put her associations and I my questions and interpretations. Ellen and I established a society of two in which we shared certain words and assumptions, although we each used them in our individual styles.

In terms of Figure 2, the lowest loop involved the look of the cartoons and the sounds Ellen and I shared. At a higher level, we were both using cultural resources plus the possibilities of our momentary community of two. At the highest level, we each had our private thoughts and interpretations.

We created data: a narrative joining her past laughing at Kliban, our present interview, and the many experiences she brought to the cartoons from a culture we share, such as college mixers, rubbing in ointments, or looking for cancer. Such a narrative forms both the data and the normal mode of psychoanalytic explanation.[11] Identity theory, in turn, provides a

way of thinking systematically about that narrative as a sequence of variations on a theme. Frankly, this interpretive process with its criteria for stronger and weaker explanations seems
to me to qualify as "scientific."

After all, this explanation of laughter rests on a general
theory of identity, which has yielded useful accounts of the
person in reading, styles of creative writing, perceiving other
people, college and secondary school teaching, the popular arts,
political choices, and psychological experimentation.[12] I realize
that in saying that Ellen's remarks reveal a general way to
understand the impulse to laugh, I am claiming a lot for one
interview, but I feel one thorough case study suffices to extend
identity theory from these other contexts to jokes and laughter.

Identity theory provides a theme-and-variations technique
that refines the traditional method of "case study." Experimental psychologists sometimes criticize the case study as a self-
fulfilling prophecy. One cannot prophesy, however, what
theme will fit together what Ellen says or how directly. The
only prophecy is that you or I will be able to read what she
says as a theme and variations, in other words, that we can
find a consistency and continuity in her actions. Any psychology begins with the same assumption, to be confirmed or disconfirmed by some psychologist's observation of some other
person's actions. Any psychology rests—or should rest—on
feedback, and an inquiry from case to case through identity
theory does.

One asks questions about an individual situation, such as
Ellen's laughing at these particular cartoons. One gets answers
that lead to a fuller understanding of that particular situation.
Those answers one can generalize into further questions, leading to closer questioning of this and similar situations, thus to
more answers that lead to more questions. And so on around
the psychologist's physical, cultural, and personal loops.

Indeed, identity theory nullifies some of the problems that
trouble conventional experimenters trying to discover psychological rules "out there," separate from the process of seeking

them. For example, just as one cannot isolate such "variables" as incongruity, one cannot separate what Ellen was saying about the cartoons from what she was saying about her parents or what she was saying for my benefit. Nor can one "control for" my "effect" on the interview. To be sure, if someone else had interviewed her, the interview would have been different. That difference would not have revealed the "effect" of a different interviewer, however. Rather, as a second psychoanalyst elicits a different transference from an analysand, another interviewer would have gotten other, different examples of Ellen's re-creation of her identity. There was no way to "control for" or "isolate" my "effect" on the interview—but no need to, because any such "effect," like any transference, would be something Ellen made through her Ellen-ness.

I could do nothing that would get Ellen to act un-Ellenly. Whatever Ellen does is, by definition, Ellenly. The instant she acts, she has added something new to the actions on which I base my questions about her identity and my definition of Ellen-ness.

The identity principle is general, but as *inquiry* rather than statement. Each answer derived from it is unique—like Ellen's highly individual laughing at Kliban—but each inquiry is the first step in a feedback that itself embodies general principles.

In the same way, the four terms, expectation, defense, fantasy, and transformation are not so much things people do as ways you and I can inquire into what they (and we) do. How did Ellen defend? Our concept of defense becomes a way we can unpack and understand the details of her response in the light of a more general theory of identity. DEFT is a way of naming processes within the social or physiological loops.

Similarly, if we think of our two hundred theories and variations of theories as providing us not with answers, but with questions, we can relate those earlier theories to an explanation of humor through identity. They let us look into Ellen's laughing for incongruity or transcendence or archetypes, just as we would look for defense or expectation. They, too, are efforts to unfold the cultural or biophysical feedback loops in laughing.

The comic thus sheds light, surprisingly, on science. For us in the arts, humor also poses a fundamental question. Given that Ellen laughs at Kliban's cartoons, why do so many others laugh at them? And why do so many not laugh?

If identity theory is right, Kliban, or for that matter Shakespeare, succeeds as an artist because, when many different individuals bring many different individualities to bear on their works, despite their differences, they succeed in recreating their identities. Traditionally, to find the key to artistic success, we have looked to the cartoon or the tragedy—the stimulus in a stimulus-response model. We hoped we could ignore the individualities of the responders and generalize simply from the stimulus. (And it certainly would be simpler!) But this analysis of Ellen's laughing tells me we çan't.

Instead of a model that moves in only one direction, artistic stimulus causing artistic response, we need to assume a transaction in which the stimulus exists in relation to a response as the response exists in relation to a stimulus. We need to look to the creative relationship between Kliban's admirers and the funniness they help to make. To discover the reason for many people's amusement, we have to consider many people.

That is a simple way of indicating a very far-reaching change in the way I think about such human experiences as laughter. I find that as I use identity theory, I place events in larger and larger scenes. For example, Hobbes's theory represents a partial, earlier version of Freud's larger but more precise theory. Hobbes says we laugh because we suddenly feel superior. Freud says we laugh because we gratify a tabooed, unconscious wish through the condensations made possible by the joke form. Among the many wishes possible for a joke to satisfy, Freud includes a fantasy of sudden glory, but Freud's theory not only includes more wishes, it shows how they all fit a total depth psychology of the individual. Freud's theory is both more general and more precise than Hobbes's.

Similarly, the DEFT theory of laughing grows from and includes Freud's theory, at the same time that it links laughing to a more general model of the way we transact texts and reality. Identity and DEFT make Freud's theory more precise by turning the powerful lens of psychoanalytic interpretation on the laugher, when Freud looked only at the joke.

To return to the very first theory of laughter we considered, Hazlitt says we laugh at a sudden incongruity. But incongruity—discrepancy—is part of the perception that brings defense into play in our DEFTing of a text. Incongruity is an earlier way of saying something that modern identity theory allows us to say in both a more exact and a more general way.

In the same way, however, while identity theory enlarges and makes precise our traditional explanations, it means we "know" personally. In one traditional view, we simply know something. That's that. Identity theory says the "I" of "I know" knows within an identity that is itself something known and relative to its knower. Thus identity decenters our knowing, indeed our very selves. The center of me includes a not-me or a semi-me, the being who interprets me. A paradox, a most ingenious paradox.

I warned you about this at the outset.

Laughing involves its theorists in their whole philosophy, or in my case (yes, "case") my whole psychology. And I use *that* word too in a double sense: the psychology of me and the psychology I believe in. How, according to identity theory, could it be otherwise? In explaining, we slowly and strugglingly recreate our identities.

In laughing, we suddenly and playfully recreate our identities. "Slowly," "strugglingly," "suddenly," "playfully," and "identities" themselves, however, are functions of our identity, and our identity in turn is a function of the identity of the person (even a moment of ourselves) construing that identity.

Identity, then, offers but one small step in a dialectical understanding of many laughings. Nevertheless, I "know"—or at least I think I know—more than I did when I began my long inquiry into laughing twenty-five years ago.

Why do we laugh? Because we are, as the children's song says,

> Free to be
> You and me.

Precisely.

Notes

The references to the first six chapters make up an extensive bibliography of theories of laughter and the comic. Rather than use conventional footnoting, then, I can be most useful by referring you to the Bibliography of Theories of Humor that follows.

Accordingly, the notes for Part I (Chapters 1–6) are keyed to the Bibliography. Authors named in the text are not also footnoted here, unless to indicate which of several passages is referred to. Footnotes for Chapters 1–6 indicate only the author's name and whatever information will focus on one item in the Bibliography. The notes for Part II (Chapters 7–11) are of the usual kind.

1. The Comic

1. See also Canetti.
2. Ecclesiastes 2:2. Pity: Grant, pp. 13–14.
3. Clarifying: Lilly; Corbyn Morris.
4. Renaissance theories: Castelvetro, Joubert, Madius, Minturno, Riccoboni, Robortello, Trissino.
5. Bibliographies: Bergler; Berlyne 1969; Ferroni; Flugel; Goldstein and McGhee 1972; Goldstein et al. 1978; Hall and Allin; Hayworth; Keith-Spiegel; Mikhail; Milner; Müller; Piddington; Smith; Treadwell; Valentine.
6. Anthologizers: of jokes, Esar; of theories, Lauter; Enck et al. Sorters: Monro; Olson; Schmidt and Williams; Rapp 1947.
7. Against definition: Cazamian.

2. Stimuli

1. Incongruity: Hunt, p. 8. Now and earlier: Menon, p. 39. Like and unlike: Beattie, George Campbell, Dennis, Flögel.
2. Affirms and denies: Dumont. Disorder: Fabre. Organization: Eastman 1921: 20–21, 25, 1936. Intellectual vs. emotional: Lévêque. Real vs. ideal: Feibleman 1939: 178–79, 1949.
3. Values: Lalo. Person as thing: Hartmann.
4. Social: Piddington. The Fool: Willeford.
5. Plato, *Philebus*. See also Mendelssohn. Invented vs. factual self: Cox.
6. Swift: see also Bullitt, p. 24. Fielding: see also Corbyn Morris. Hypocrisy: Oliver. Excellence: Kronenberger, p. 3; Corrigan, p. xiii.
7. Specialization: Scott. Conventions: Monro.
8. Perception, means: Smith, p. 63. High and low: Flögel.
9. Idealist view: Vischer.
10. Admiration: Akenside. Plausibility: Mélinand.
11. Play: Saulnier, p. 174.
12. Defect: Sully, p. 139. Little thing: Lipps, p. 575.
13. See also Olson, p. 23: "a minimization of the claim . . . to be taken seriously."
14. See also Maier; Fry 1963.
15. Circumstances: Ribot. Analysis of text: Knights.

3. Conditions

1. Play generally: Eastman 1936.
2. For Brooks, see Tynan, p. 94.
3. Objectivity, isolation: Maier. Compactness, mechanism, exaggeration: Schoeller.
4. See Koestler 1949: 110.
5. Sixteenth century: Madius, pp. 323–24. Sustained humor: Koestler 1949.
6. Hamlet: see Eberhart.

4. Psychology

1. Freud 1913; Frye 1957: 35–52.
2. Cornford, chaps. 4 and 5.
3. Initiation: Thomson. Invective: Aristotle, *Poetics*, cap. 4. Satire: Elliott.
4. Frye 1949: 64.
5. "Comic resolution": Frye 1949: 65. Satyr play: Kerr, p. 25.
6. Frye 1949: 64, 1957: 35–52.
7. *Felix culpa*: Weisinger. *Commedia*: Frye 1949: 65.
8. Characters: Frye 1957: 39–48. Scapegoats survive: Welsford. Aristotle: *Ethics*, bk. 4, cap. 8.
9. Silent woman: Cornford, chaps. 7 and 8.

10. Platonic dialogues: Greene. Aristotle, *Poetics*, cap. 5.

11. Chambers, I, 317.

12. Sypher, p. 221.

13. Comic license: Goodman. Comic purgations: Barber.

14. Isaiah 61:10–11.

15. Levy.

16. Cornford, chaps. 7 and 8.

17. Langer, pp. 331 and 344.

18. "Expected": Müller, p. 137. Body: Gregory. Safety: Hayworth.

19. Willmann.

20. French theorist: Aubouin, p. 260; Berlyne 1960: 259.

21. Priestley, p. 200.

22. "The passion": Hobbes 1650. Laughs too much: Hobbes 1651.

23. Satire and caricature: Kris, p. 183. Animal enraged: Ludovici.

24. Addison, II, 465. Malign pleasure: Lamennais. Manners: Marmontel. See also Sidis.

25. Identification: Bain. Effectance: White. General principle: Jünger.

26. Burke 1937; quotation from Burke 1941.

27. "Frustrated menace": Kallen 1910: 137. Liberation: Kallen 1968: 59.

28. Eighteenth century: Hartley. Tickling: Eastman 1936. Psychoanalytic: Kris, p. 215.

29. *Punch*: Muggeridge. Sympathy: McDougall 1922a, 1922b. Anger: Rapp 1951: 169. Anthropologists: Radcliffe-Brown 1949, 1952.

30. Leacock, p. 11. Others: L. W. Kline; Repplier, p. 5. See also Nicolson.

31. Kris, p. 208.

32. Chap. 7, sec. 3, p. 209.

33. Eastman 1936.

34. "Freudian" symbolism: Grotjahn 1957. Ambivalence: Greig, p. 66. See also Trachtenberg.

35. Comedy: Turk. Gestalt: Ehrenzweig. Chomsky: Bradshaw. Experiment: Paul Kline 1978.

36. Patients: Grotjahn 1969. Therapist: Nicholi, pp. 16–17.

37. Kris, chaps. 6–9.

38. Gesell, Washburn.

39. Rothbart 1978: 92–93.

40. Observer Wit Tally: Goodchilds. Multiple causes: Foot and Chapman, Giles and Oxford.

41. Scale: Rothbart 1978: 93. Laryngograph: Mair and Kirkland.

42. Branch et al.

43. Summaries: Perl; Treadwell; Goldstein and McGhee 1972: chap. 13. The "big" book: Chapman and Foot 1978. Its bibliography: Goldstein et al.

44. In so doing I am relying heavily on the incisive surveys by Rothbart and by Leventhal and Safer in Chapman and Foot 1978.

45. Pupil dilation: Wagoner and Sullenberger. Height: Stump. Traffic: Kole and Henderson. Dieting: Leventhal and Safer, p. 346.

46. IC: La Fave; Zillmann and Cantor. "Necessary ingredients": La Fave et al., p. 89.

47. Men and women: O'Connell 1962; Eysenck 1943. Aggressive jokes: Murray. Mental patients: Roberts and Johnson. Extroverts: Eysenck 1942.

48. Subdividing Freud: O'Connell 1964. 100 jokes: Cattell and Luborsky.

49. WHAT: O'Connell 1962. MRT: Redlich et al. IPAT: Cattell and Tollefson.

50. Cartoon responses: Levine. See also Levine and Abelson; Levine and Redlich 1955, 1960.

51. Eysenck 1972.

52. Castell and Goldstein; Shultz 1978.

53. Morrison.

54. Pollio, p. 776; Pollio and Edgerly; Murphy and Pollio.

55. Ambrose 1960, 1961; McGhee 1971, 1978b, 1979.

56. Act vs. situation: Justin. Shouting: Seward.

57. Stimulus maintaining or terminating: Blatz et al., p. 27. Adaptive: Sroufe and Wunsch.

58. Leventhal and Safer, pp. 339–41; Rothbart 1976.

59. Berlyne 1960. See also Godkewitsch.

60. Two stages: Suls; see also Shultz 1976. "Difficult": Rothbart 1978: 91.

61. Sophomores: Nerhardt 1970, 1976. Children: Shultz and Horibe. See the summary in Rothbart 1978: 91.

62. Apter and Smith.

63. Rothbart 1978: 92.

64. Leventhal and Safer, p. 342.

65. Heim; Hellyar.

66. See, for example, Paul Kline 1972: 194–200; McGhee 1971; McGhee and Goldstein; Rothbart 1978; Leventhal and Safer.

67. Pagnol, pp. 17, 124; Potts, p. 45.

5. Physiology

1. Muscles: Rauleir. Smiling: Critchley, pp. 40–41.

2. Koestler 1949.

3. Diseases: Nicholi, pp. 34, 70, 72, 211, 309, and 315. Alzheimer, Pick, kuru, gelastic epilepsy, epidemics: Critchley, pp. 40–41.

4. Rauleir.

5. Cited by Critchley, pp. 40–41.

6. Koestler 1964: 59, 95.

7. Madius, pp. 323–24. Physiologist: Crile, pp. 332ff.

8. Psychoanalytic: Greig, p. 66. Non-Freudian: McDougall 1922a, 1922b, 1926: 165.

9. Canetti.

10. Koestler 1964: 58.

11. Cooperation: McComas. Vocal signal: Hayworth. Adjustment: Piddington. Disguise: Meerloo.

12. Metacommunicative signal: Van Hooff. Appeasement: Fry 1978.

13. Infant's smile: Ambrose 1960, 1961.
14. McGhee 1979: 121–22.
15. McGhee and Goldstein, p. 249.

6. Catharsis

1. See, for example, Bullitt, p. 8.
2. Psychologists: see the survey in Rothbart 1978: 90. Sociologist: Scheff. See also Wilson.
3. Recently: Mindess.
4. Burke 1937: I, 52; Frye 1949: 66, 1957: 169–70. Golden mean: Cook. Group: Dupreel. Purposes of teller: Kane et al. Cognitive, social: Foss.
5. Social norm: Potts, p. 45. Semioticist: Milner, p. 27.
6. Radliffe-Brown 1940, 1949, 1952. Cf. Rigby.
7. The quotations: Douglas 1968: 336, 365, 370, 373, 375. "Ritual purifier": Douglas 1975: 107.
8. Kerr, p. 28. Ideas: Flögel, I, 55. Moment of logical truth: Swabey, p. v.
9. Vos, pp. 13, 7, 114.
10. Feibleman 1949.
11. Graves, p. 55. Representing God: Carrit. Without God: Holmer.
12. Kierkegaard; quotations from pp. 77, 287, 82, 533, and 83.
13. More-than-human: Kindermann.

7. Theorists Theorizing

1. Berlyne 1971: 4.

8. Laughers Laughing

1. *New York Times*, February 12, 1978, sec. 1, p. 56. For a more personal reading of Kliban (and the variability of response to his cartoons), see Charles M. Young, "B. Kliban: Terrors of the Universe and Other Cartoons," *Rolling Stone*, September 21, 1978, pp. 34–37.
2. New York: Workman, 1976.

9. Identity

1. Heinz Lichtenstein, "Identity and Sexuality" (1961), in *The Dilemma of Human Identity* (New York: Jason Aronson, 1977), pp. 49–126.
2. Paul Diesing, *Patterns of Discovery in the Social Sciences* (Chicago: Aldine-Atherton, 1971), pp. 5–6. For more on the philosophical issues involved, see the discussion of Arthur Koestler's *Ghost in the Machine* (1967) in D. C. Phillips, *Holistic Thought in Social Science* (Stanford: Stanford University Press, 1976), pp. 68–75. Identity theory is an instance of Phillips' "Holism 3."
3. Larry R. Baas and Steven R. Brown, "Generating Rules for Intensive

Analysis: The Study of Transformations," *Psychiatry*, 36 (1973), 172–83, 173.

4. "Remarks on the Theory and Practice of Dream-Interpretation" (1923), in *Standard Edition*, xix, 116. See also *Moses and Monotheism* (1939), Chap. 2, in ibid.; xxiii, 17.

5. *"The Aetiology of Hysteria"* (1896), in *Standard Edition*, iii, 192. See also "Constructions in Analysis" (1937), in ibid.; xxiii, 259–60.

6. René Wellek, "Closing Statement," in *Style in Language*, ed. Thomas A. Sebeok (Cambridge, Mass.: M.I.T. Press, 1960), p. 419.

10. Why Ellen Laughed

1. Norman N. Holland and Murray M. Schwartz, "The Delphi Seminar," *College English*, 36 (1975), 789–800.

11. Why the Rest of Us Laugh

1. Lawrence La Fave et al., pp. 84–85.

2. George Lakoff and Mark Johnson (*Metaphors We Live By* [Chicago: University of Chicago Press, 1980]) point out a great many families of metaphors that shape or reflect fundamental attitudes: abstractions as persons, for example ("the university refused"), or places ("the White House"), or adversaries ("inflation is our biggest enemy"). They argue persuasively that one should regard such metaphors as a necessary route to understanding the world by interacting with it. My discussion from here to the end of this book proceeds from that assumption: that we best understand the world by making our metaphors (including our scientific metaphors) as enlightening as we can.

3. William T. Powers, *Behavior: The Control of Perception* (Chicago: Aldine, 1973). Also by Powers: "Feedback: Beyond Behaviorism," *Science*, 179 (1973), 351–56; "Quantitative Analysis of Purposive Systems: Some Spadework at the Foundations of Scientific Psychology," *Psychological Review*, 85 (1978), 417–35.

4. *Standard Edition*, V, 565–66.

5. *Jokes and Their Relation to the Unconscious*, in *Standard Edition*, VIII, 151, 99, and 100.

6. I have developed this concept at somewhat greater length in *5 Readers Reading* (New Haven: Yale University Press, 1975), pp. 233–46.

7. Jan B. Deregowski, "Difficulties in Depth Perception in Africa," *British Journal of Psychology*, 59 (1968), 195–204.

8. Colin Turnbull, "Some Observations Regarding the Experiences and Behavior of the BaMbuti Pygmies," *American Journal of Psychology*, 74 (1961), 304–8.

9. For a variety of these effects, see Robert L. and Ruth H. Munroe, *Cross-Cultural Human Development* (Monterey: Brooks/Cole, 1975), pp. 67–70; Marshall H. Segall, Donald T. Campbell, and Melville J. Herskovits, *The Influence of Culture on Visual Perception* (Indianapolis: Bobbs-Merrill,

1966); Barbara B. Lloyd, *Perception and Cognition: A Cross-Cultural Perspective* (London: Penguin, 1972).

10. Thomas Kuhn's justifiably well-known *Structure of Scientific Revolutions* (Chicago: University of Chicago Press, 1962) shows how scientists "do" normal science in accordance with a prevailing scientific culture or break out of that culture for radical innovations. Stanley Fish has recently shown the same sort of thing in the teaching and criticism of literature: *Is There a Text in This Class?: The Authority of Interpretive Communities* (Cambridge: Harvard University Press, 1980).

11. Michael Sherwood, *The Logic of Explanation in Psychoanalysis* (New York and London: Academic Press, 1969).

12. A number of works emanating directly or indirectly from the Center for the Psychological Study of the Arts at the State University of New York at Buffalo have applied identity theory to explain the personal element in various human activities:

Reading: Norman N. Holland, *5 Readers Reading*.

Creative styles: Holland, *Poems in Persons* (New York: Norton, 1973), referring to Hilda Doolittle; Murray M. Schwartz and Christopher Bollas, "The Absence at the Center: Sylvia Plath and Suicide," *Criticism*, 18 (1976), 147–72; Murray M. Schwartz, "D. H. Lawrence and Psychoanalysis: An Introduction," *D. H. Lawrence Review*, 10 (1977), 215–22; Gregory R. Zeck, "Hart Crane's *The Wine Menagerie*," *American Imago*, 36 (1980), 197–214.

Perceiving other people: Holland and Schwartz, "The Delphi Seminar," *College English*, 36 (1975) 789–800.

College teaching: ibid.; English 692, "Poem Opening: An Invitation to Transactive Criticism," *College English*, 40 (1978), 2–16.

Secondary school teaching: Anthony R. Petrosky, "Individual and Group Responses of Fourteen and Fifteen Year Olds to Short Stories, Novels, Poems, and Thematic Apperception Tests: Case Studies Based on Piagetian Genetic Epistemology and Freudian Psychoanalytic Ego Psychology," *DAI*, 36 (1975), 75–76, 956A (State University of New York at Buffalo); Agnes Webb, "Research Conducted in Schools: A Report of a Study of Response to Literature and a Reconsideration of the Proposal for the Study," paper presented to the Buffalo Conference on Researching Response to Literature and the Teaching of Literature, October 27–29, 1977, State University of New York at Buffalo, Department of English Education.

The popular arts: Roger B. Rollin, "Against Evaluation: The Role of the Critic in Popular Literature," *Journal of Popular Culture*, 9 (1975), 355–65; Nathan Paramathan, "Television Themes and Styles—an Application of N. Holland's Transformation Theory," *Melbourne Journal of Politics*, 10 (1978), 51–64.

Political choice: Graham Little, *Politics and Personal Style* (Melbourne: Thomas Nelson, 1973).

Psychological experimentation: Norman N. Holland, "Identity: An Interrogation at the Border of Psychology," *Language and Style*, 10 (1977), 199–209.

Bibliography of Theories
of Humor

Addison, Joseph. *The Spectator*. Ed. Donald F. Bond. 2 vols. Oxford, 1965. II, 465–66.

Akenside, Mark. *Pleasures of the Imagination* (1744). Note to 3.248.

Ambrose, J. A. "The Smiling and Related Responses in Early Human Infancy: An Experimental and Theoretical Study of Their Course and Significance." Diss. Birkbeck College, London University, 1960.

———. "The Development of the Smiling Response in Early Infancy." In *Determinants of Infant Behaviour*, ed. B. M. Foss. London and New York, 1961.

Apter, Michael J., and K. C. P. Smith. "Humour and the Theory of Psychological Reversals." In Chapman and Foot (1978), pp. 95–100.

Aristophanes. *The Frogs* (405 B.C.), particularly 1472–1526.

Aristotle. (fl. 367–322 B.C.). *Poetics*. Trans. S. H. Butcher. Caps. 2, 4, 5, 6.

———. *Ethics*. Trans. J. A. K. Thomson. Bk. IV, cap. 8.

———. *Parts of Animals*. Trans. A. L. Peck. III.x.373a.

Aubouin, Elie. *Technique et psychologie du comique*. Marseilles, 1948.

Auden, W. H. "Notes on the Comic." In *The Dyer's Hand and Other Essays*. New York, 1962. Pp. 371–85.

Bain, Alexander. *The Emotions and the Will*. London, 1865. Chap. 14.

Barber, C. L. *Shakespeare's Festive Comedy: A Study of Dramatic Form and Its Relation to Social Custom*. Princeton, N.J., 1959.

Bateson, Gregory. "The Position of Humor in Human Communication." In *Cybernetics: Circular Causal and Feedback Mechanisms in Biological and Social Sciences*, Transactions of the Ninth Conference on Cybernetics, ed. Heinz von Foerster. New York, 1953. Pp. 1–47.

Baudelaire, Charles. "On the Essence of Laughter, and in General, On the Comic in the Plastic Arts" (1855). Trans. Gerard Hopkins.

Beattie, James. "Essay on Laughter and Ludicrous Composition." In *Essays*, 3d ed., 1779.

Beerbohm, Max. "Laughter." In *And Even Now*. London, 1920.

Bergler, Edmund. *Laughter and the Sense of Humor*. New York, 1956.

Bergson, Henri. *Laughter* (1900). In *Comedy*, ed. Wylie Sypher. Garden City, 1956. Pp. 67, 64–65.

Berlyne, D. E. *Conflict, Arousal, and Curiosity*. New York, 1960. Pp. 253–61.

———. "Laughter, Humor, and Play." In *The Handbook of Social Psychology*, 2d ed., ed. Gardner Lindzey and Elliott Aronson. Reading, Mass., 1969. III, 795–852.

———. *Aesthetics and Psychobiology* New York: Appleton-Century-Crofts, 1971.

———. "Humor and Its Kin." In Goldstein and McGhee (1972), pp. 43–60.

Blatz, William E., Kathleen Drew Allin, and Dorothy A. Millichamp. *A Study of Laughter in the Nursery School Child*. University of Toronto Studies, Child Development Series, no. 7. Toronto, 1936.

Bradshaw, John. "Verbal Jokes as De-Transformed Utterances and as Speech Acts." In Chapman and Foot (1978), pp. 61–64.

Branch, A. Y., G. A. Fine, and J. M. Jones. "Laughter, Smiling, and Rating Scales: An Analysis of Responses to Tape-Recorded Humor." *Proceedings of the American Psychological Association*, 8 (1973), 189–90.

Bullitt, John M. *Jonathan Swift and the Anatomy of Satire*. Cambridge, Mass., 1953.

Burke, Kenneth. *Attitudes toward History*. 2 vols. New York, 1937. I, 51–54.

———. "Hypergelasticism Exposed." In *The Philosophy of Literary Form*. Baton Rouge, 1941.

Campbell, George. *Philosophy of Rhetoric* (1776). I, 87.

Campbell, Joseph. "Tragedy and Comedy." In *The Hero of a Thousand Faces*. New York, 1949. Pp. 25–30.

Canetti, Elias. *Crowds and Power*. Trans. Carol Stewart. New York, 1962. Pp. 223–24.

Capp, Al. "The Comedy of Charlie Chaplin." *Atlantic Monthly*, 185 (1950), 25–29.

Carlyle, Thomas. "Jean Paul Friedrich Richter." *Edinburgh Review*, 91 (1827).

Carrit, E. F. "A Theory of the Ludicrous." *Hibbert Journal*, 21 (1923), 552–64.

Cassirer, Ernst. "Art." In *An Essay on Man*. New Haven, 1944. P. 192.

Castell, Patricia J., and Jeffrey H. Goldstein. "Social Occasions for Joking: A Cross-Cultural Study." In Chapman and Foot (1978), pp. 193–97.

Castelvetro, Lodovico. *Commentary on Aristotle's "Poetics"* (1570).

Cattell, Raymond B., and Lester B. Luborsky. "Personality Factors in Response to Humor." *Journal of Abnormal and Social Psychology*, 42 (1947), 402–21.

——— and Donald L. Tollefson. *The IPAT [Institute for Personality and Ability Testing] Humor Test of Personality*. Champaign, Ill., 1966.

Cazamian, Louis. "Pourquoi nous ne pouvons définir l'humour." *Revue Germanique*, November–December 1906, p. 629.

Cervantes, Miguel de. *Don Quixote* (1605, 1615). Pt. II, chap. xii.

Chambers, E. K. *The Medieval Stage*. 2 vols. London, 1903.

Chapman, Antony J., and Hugh C. Foot, eds. *Humour and Laughter: Theory, Research, and Applications*. London, 1976.

——— and ———, eds. *It's a Funny Thing, Humour*. Oxford, 1978.

Chaucer, Geoffrey. *Troilus and Criseyde* (1386). V, 1786–1869.

Chesterfield, Philip Dormer Stanhope, 4th Earl of. *Letters to His Son*. London, 1774. March 9, 1748.

Cicero. *De Oratore* (55 B.C.). II, 58, 236.

Clynes, Manfred. *Sentics: The Touch of the Emotions*. Garden City, N.Y., 1977. Pp. 207–12.

Coleridge, Samuel Taylor. "On Wit and Humor." In *Coleridge's Miscellaneous Criticism*, ed. Thomas M. Raysor. London, 1936.

Congreve, William. "Concerning Humour in Comedy" (1695). In *Critical Essays of the Seventeenth Century*, ed. Joel E. Spingarn, 3 vols. Oxford, 1908.

Cook, Albert S. *The Dark Voyage and the Golden Mean*. Cambridge, Mass., 1949.

Cooper, Lane. *An Aristotelian Theory of Comedy*. New York, 1922.

Cornford, Francis M. *The Origin of Attic Comedy*. London, 1914.

Corrigan, Robert W., ed. *Comedy: A Critical Anthology*. Boston, 1971.

Cousins, Norman. "Anatomy of an Illness (as Perceived by the Patient)." *New England Journal of Medicine*, 295 (1976), 1458–63.

Cox, Roger L. "The Invented Self: An Essay on Comedy." *Soundings*, 57 (1974), 139–56.

Crile, G. W. *Man—An Adaptive Mechanism*. New York, 1916. Pp. 332ff.

Critchley, Macdonald. *Silent Language*. London, 1975. Pp. 40–41.

Croce, Benedetto. *Aesthetic*. Trans. Douglas Ainslee. 2d ed. London, 1922. P. 92.

Darwin, Charles. *The Expression of the Emotions in Man and Animals* (1872). Chap. 8.

Dennis, John. "Remarks on Mr. Pope's 'Rape of the Lock'" (1714). In *Critical Works*, ed. Edward Niles Hooker, 2 vols. Baltimore, 1939. II, 331.

Descartes, René. *Les passions de l'âme* (1649). Arts. 124–27.

Dewey, John. "The Theory of Emotion." *Psychological Review*, 1 (1894), no. 6.

Donatus, Ælius. *De Comædia et Tragœdia* (c. A.D. 350).

Douglas, Mary. "The Social Control of Cognition: Some Factors in Joke Perception." *Man*, n.s. 3 (1968), 361–76.

———. "Jokes" and "Do Dogs Laugh? A Cross-Cultural Approach to Body Symbolism." In *Implicit Meanings: Essays in Anthropology*. London, 1975. Pp. 83–89 and 90–114.

Dryden, John. Preface to *An Evening's Love* (1671).

Dumont, Léon. *Des causes du rire*. Paris, 1862.

Dupreel, P. "The Sociology of Laughter." *Revue Philosophique*, 106 (1928), 213–60.

Eastman, Max. *The Sense of Humor*. New York, 1921.

———. *The Enjoyment of Laughter*. New York, 1936.

Eberhart, Richard. "Tragedy as Limitation: Comedy as Control and Resolution." *Tulane Drama Review*, 6 (1962), 3–14.

Ehrenzweig, Anton. "The Inarticulate ('Baffling') Structure of the Joke." In *The Psycho-Analysis of Artistic Vision and Hearing: An Introduction to a Theory of Artistic Perception*, 2d ed. New York, 1965. Chap. 8.

Elliott, Robert C. "The Satirist and Society." *English Literary History*, 21 (1954), 237–48.

Ellis, Havelock. *Studies in the Psychology of Sex* (1899–1928). 2 vols. New York, 1942. Vol. I, pt. 3, pp. 11–18.

Emerson, Ralph Waldo. "The Comic." In *Letters and Social Aims* (1883).

Enck, John J., Elizabeth T. Forter, and Alvin Whitley. *The Comic in Theory and Practice*. New York, 1960.

Epictetus. *Discourses* (c. A.D. 90). Trans. George Long. Bk. 1, chap. 4, 109d.

Esar, Evan. *The Humor of Humor*. New York, 1952.

Eysenck, H. J. "Appreciation of Humor—an Experimental and Theoretical Study." *British Journal of Psychology*, 32 (1942), 295–309.

———. "An Experimental Analysis of Five Tests of 'Appreciation of Humor.'" *Educational and Psychological Measurement*, 3 (1943), 191–214.

———. "Foreword." In Goldstein and McGhee (1972), pp. xiii–xvii.

Fabre, Lucien. *Le rire et les rieurs*. Paris, 1929.

Feibleman, James. *In Praise of Comedy*. New York, 1939.

———. "The Meaning of Comedy." In *Aesthetics*, ed. J. Stolnitz. Chicago, 1949. Chap. 5.

Ferroni, Giulio. *Il Comico nelle teorie contemporanee*. Rome, 1974.

Fielding, Henry. Preface to *Joseph Andrews* (1742).

Fisher, Seymour, and Rhoda L. Fisher. *Pretend the World Is Funny and Forever: A Psychological Analysis of Comedians, Clowns, and Actors*. Hillsdale, N.J., 1981.

Flögel, Carl Friedrich. *Geshichte der Komischen Literatur*. Leipzig, 1784.

Flugel, J. C. "Humor and Laughter." In *Handbook of Social Psychology*, ed. Gardner Lindzey. Reading, Mass., 1954. II, 709–34.

Foot, Hugh C., and Antony J. Chapman. "The Social Responsiveness of Young Children in Humorous Situations." In Chapman and Foot (1976), pp. 188–214.

Foss, B. M. "Foreword." In Chapman and Foot (1978), pp. xiii–xiv.

Freud, Sigmund. *Jokes and Their Relation to the Unconscious* (1905). In *Standard Edition of the Complete Psychological Works of Sigmund Freud*, trans. James Strachey et al., ed. James Strachey. 24 vols. London: Hogarth Press, 1953–74. VIII.

———. *Totem and Taboo* (1913). *Standard Edition*, XIII, ix–162.

———. "Humour" (1927). *Standard Edition*, XXI, 159–66.

Fry, William. *Sweet Madness: A Study of Humor*. Palo Alto, Calif., 1963.

———. "The Appeasement Function of Mirthful Laughter." In Chapman and Foot (1978), pp. 23–26.

Frye, Northrop C. "The Argument of Comedy." In *English Institute Essays, 1948*, ed. D. A. Robertson, Jr. New York, 1949.

———. *Anatomy of Criticism: Four Essays*. Princeton, N.J., 1957.

Gesell, Arnold. *The Mental Growth of the Pre-School Child*. New York, 1925.

Giles, Howard, and G. S. Oxford. "Towards a Multidimensional Theory of Laughter Causation and Its Social Implications." *Bulletin of the British Psychological Society*, 22 (1970), 97–105.

Girard, René. "Perilous Balance: A Comic Hypothesis." *Modern Language Notes*, 87 (1972), 811–26.

Godkewitsch, Michael. "Physiological and Verbal Indices of Arousal in Rated Humour." In Chapman and Foot (1976), pp. 117–38.

Goldstein, Jeffrey H., and Paul E. McGhee. "An Annotated Bibliography of Published Papers on Humor in the Research Literature and an Analysis of Trends: 1900–1971." In Goldstein and McGhee (1972), pp. 263–83.

——— and ———, eds. *The Psychology of Humor*. New York, 1972.

——— and ———, Jean R. Smith, Antony J. Chapman, and Hugh C. Foot. "Humour, Laughter, and Comedy: A Bibliography of Empirical and Nonempirical Analyses in the English Language." In Chapman and Foot (1978), pp. 469–504.

Goodchilds, Jacqueline D. "On Being Witty: Causes, Correlates, and Consequences." In Goldstein and McGhee (1972), pp. 173–93.

Goodman, Paul. "Comic Plots." *The Structure of Literature*. Chicago, 1954. Chap. 3.

Grant, Mary A. *The Ancient Rhetorical Theories of the Laughable*. University of Wisconsin Studies in Language and Literature, no. 21. Madison, Wis., 1924.

Graves, Robert. *Mrs. Fisher, or the Future of Humour*. London, 1928.

Greene, William Chace. "The Spirit of Comedy in Plato." *Harvard Studies in Classical Philology*, 31 (1920), 63–123.

Gregory, J. C. *The Nature of Laughter*. London, 1924.

Greig, J. Y. T. *The Psychology of Laughter and Comedy*. London, 1923.

Grotjahn, Martin. *Beyond Laughter*. New York, 1957.

———. "Laughter and Sex." *Human Sexuality*, 3 (1969), 92–96.

Hall, G. Stanley, and Arthur Allin. "The Psychology of Tickling, Laughing, and the Comic." *American Journal of Psychology*, 9 (1897), 1–41.

Hartley, David. *Observations on Man* (1749). Pt. 1, chap. 4.

Hartmann, Robert S. Personal communication.

Hayworth, Donald. "The Social Origin and Function of Laughter." *Psychological Review*, 35 (1928), 367–84.

Hazlitt, William. "On Wit and Humour." *Lectures on the English Comic Writers* (1819). Lecture 1.

Hegel, G. W. F. *Aesthetik* (1819). "Dramatic Poetry," sec. 3, and "Final Summary."

Heim, A. "An Experiment on Humour." *British Journal of Psychology*, 27 (1936), 148–61.

Hellyar, Richmond H. "Laughter and Jollity." *Contemporary Review*, 132 (1927), 757–63.

Hobbes, Thomas. *Treatise of Human Nature* (1650). Chap. 9, pt. 13.2.

———. *Leviathan* (1651). Pt. 1, chap. 6.

Holland, Norman N. *Poems in Persons: An Introduction to the Psychoanalysis of Literature*. New York, 1973. Pp. 128–30.

Holmer, Paul. "Something about What Makes It Funny." *Soundings*, 57 (1974), 157–74.

Huizinga, Johann. *Homo Ludens*. London, 1944. Chap. 1 and generally.

Hunt, Leigh. *Wit and Humour*. 2d ed. London, 1848.

Hutcheson, Francis. *Reflections upon Laughter and Remarks upon the Fable of the Bees* (1725). In *Collected Works*, ed. Bernhard Fabian. Hildesheim, 1971. VII, 121 and 127.

Jacobson, Edith. "The Child's Laughter: Theoretical and Clinical Notes on the Function of the Comic." *Psychoanalytic Study of the Child*, 2 (1946), 39–60.

Jekels, Ludwig. "On the Psychology of Comedy" (1926). In *Selected Papers*. New York, 1952. Pp. 97–104.

Johnson, Samuel. *The Rambler*, no. 125 (May 28, 1751).

Joubert, Laurent. *Traité du ris* (1579). Published in English as *Treatise on Laughter*, trans. Gregory David de Rocher. University, Alabama, 1980.

Jünger, Friedrich George. *Über das Komische*. Frankfurt, 1948.

Justin, Florence. "A Genetic Study of Laughter-Provoking Stimuli." *Child Development*, 3–4 (1932–33), 114–36.

Kallen, Horace M. "The Aesthetic Principle in Comedy." *American Journal of Psychology*, 22 (1910), 137–59.

———. *Liberty, Laughter, and Tears: Reflections on the Relations of Comedy and Tragedy to Human Freedom*. DeKalb, Ill., 1968.

Kane, Thomas R., Jerry Suls, and James T. Tedeschi. "Humour as a

Tool of Social Interaction." In Chapman and Foot (1978), pp. 13–16.

Kant, Immanuel. *Critique of Judgment* (1790). Trans. J. H. Bernard. Bk. 2, sec. 54.

Keith-Spiegel, Patricia. "Early Conceptions of Humor: Varieties and Issues." In Goldstein and McGhee (1972), pp. 3–39.

Kerr, Walter. *Tragedy and Comedy*. New York, 1967.

Kierkegaard, Søren. *Concluding Unscientific Postscript* (1846). Trans. David F. Swenson and Walter Lowrie. Princeton, N.J., 1944.

Kindermann, Heinz. *Meister der Komödie*. Vienna, 1952. Chap. 1.

Kline, L. W. "The Psychology of Humor." *American Journal of Psychology*, 18 (1907), 421–44.

Kline, Paul. *Fact and Fantasy in Freudian Theory*. London, 1972.

——. "The Psychoanalytic Theory of Humour and Laughter." In Chapman and Foot (1978), pp. 7–12.

Knights, L. C. "Notes on Comedy." In *The Importance of Scrutiny*. Ed. Eric Bentley. New York, 1964.

Koestler, Arthur. *Insight and Outlook*. New York, 1949. Pt. 1.

——. *The Act of Creation*. New York, 1964.

Kole, Theodore, and Harold L. Henderson. "Cartoon Reaction Scale with Special Reference to Driving Behavior." *Journal of Applied Psychology*, 50, (1966), 311–16.

Kris, Ernst. *Psychoanalytic Explorations in Art*. New York, 1952.

Kronenberger, Louis. "Some Prefatory Words on Comedy." In *The Thread of Laughter*. New York, 1952.

La Fave, Lawrence. "Humor Judgments as a Function of Reference Groups and Identification Classes." In Goldstein and McGhee (1972), pp. 195–210.

——, Jay Haddad, and William A. Maesen. "Superiority, Enhanced Self-Esteem, and Perceived Incongruity Humour Theory." In Chapman and Foot (1976), pp. 63–91.

Lalo, Charles. *Esthétique du rire*. Paris, 1949.

Lamennais, Félicité Robert de. *Esquisse d'une philosophie*. Paris, 1840. III, ix, 2, pp. 368–75.

Langer, Susanne K. "Great Dramatic Forms: The Comic Rhythm." In *Feeling and Form*. New York, 1953. Chap. 18.

Lauter, Paul. *Theories of Comedy*. Garden City, N.Y., 1964.

Leacock, Stephen. *Humour and Humanity: An Introduction to the Study of Humour*. New York, 1938.

Lessing, Gotthold Ephraim. *Hamburgische Dramaturgie* (1769). Trans. Helen Zimmern. No. 29.

Leventhal, Howard, and Martin A. Safer. "Individual Differences, Personality, and Humour Appreciation: Introduction to Symposium." In Chapman and Foot (1978), pp. 335–49.

Lévêque, Charles. "Le rire, le comique et le risible dans l'esprit et dans l'art." *Revue des Deux Mondes*, 47 (1863), 107.

Levine, Jacob. "Responses to Humor." *Scientific American*, 194 (1953), 31–35.

—— and Robert Abelson. "Humor as a Disturbing Stimulus." *Journal of General Psychology*, 60 (1959), 191–200.

—— and Fred C. Redlich. "Failure to Understand Humor." *Psychoanalytic Quarterly*, 24 (1955), 560–72.

—— and ——. "Intellectual and Emotional Factors in the Appreciation of Humor." *Journal of Genetic Psychology*, 62 (1960), 25–35.

Levy, Gertrude Rachel. *The Gate of Horn*. London, 1948.

Lilly, W. S. "The Theory of the Ludicrous." *Fortnightly Review*, n.s. 59 (1896), 724–37.

Lipps, Theodore. *Grundlegung der Aesthetik* (1903). P. 575.

Lorenz, Konrad. *On Aggression*. New York, 1966.

Ludovici, Anthony M. *The Secret of Laughter*. New York, 1932.

McComas, H. C. "The Origin of Laughter." *Psychological Review*, 30 (1923), 45–55.

McDougall, William. "Why Do We Laugh?" *Scribner's*, 71 (1922a), 359–63.

——. "A New Theory of Laughter." *Psyche*, 2 (1922b), 292–303.

——. *Outline of Abnormal Psychology*. New York, 1926. P. 165.

McGhee, Paul E. "Development of the Humor Response: A Review of the Literature." *Psychological Bulletin*, 76 (1971), 328–48.

—— (1978a). "A Model of the Origins and Early Development of Incongruity-Based Humour." In Chapman and Foot (1978), pp. 27–36.

—— (1978b). "Children's Humour: A Review of Current Research Trends." In Chapman and Foot (1978), pp. 199–209.

——. *Humor: Its Origin and Development*. San Francisco, 1979.

—— and Jeffrey H. Goldstein. "Advances toward an Understanding of Humor: Implications for the Future." In Goldstein and McGhee (1972), pp. 243–57.

Mack, Maynard. Introduction to Henry Fielding, *Joseph Andrews*. New York, 1948.

Madius, Vincentius. *De Ridiculis* [published with his commentary on Aristotle's *Poetics*] (1550).

Maier, N. R. F. "A Gestalt Theory of Humor." *British Journal of Psychology*, 23 (1932), 69–74.

Mair, Michael, and John Kirkland. "Mirth Measurement: A New Technique." In Chapman and Foot (1978), pp. 105–11.

Marmontel, Jean François. *Encyclopédie ou dictionnaire raisonné des sciences, des arts, et des métiers*. Ed. Denis Diderot and Jean d'Alembert. Paris, 1751. S.vv. Comédie, Comique.

Marx, Karl. "A Contribution to the Critique of Hegel's 'Philosophy of Right': Introduction" (1844). Published in English as *Critique of Hegel's "Philosophy of Right,"* ed. Joseph O'Malley, trans. Annette Jolin and Joseph O'Malley. Cambridge, Mass., 1970. P. 134.

Mauron, Charles. *Psychocritique du genre comique*. Paris, 1964. Pp. 136 and 180.

Meerloo, Joost A. M. "The Biology of Laughter." *Psychoanalytic Review*, 53 (1966), 189–208.

Mélinand, C. "Pourquoi rit-on?" *Revue des Deux Mondes*, 1895.

Mendelssohn, Moses. *Gesammelte Schriften*. Leipzig, 1843. I, 256–57.

Menon, V. K. Krishna. *A Theory of Laughter*. London, 1931.

Meredith, George. *The Idea of Comedy and the Uses of the Comic Spirit*. London, 1877.

Mikhail, E. H. *Comedy and Tragedy: A Bibliography of Critical Studies*. Troy, N.Y., 1972.

Milner, G. B. "Homo Ridens: Towards a Semiotic Theory of Laughter." *Semiotica*, 5 (1972), 1–30.

Mindess, Harvey. *Laughter and Liberation*. Los Angeles, 1971.

Minturno, Antonio Sebastiano. *The Art of Poetry* (1563).

Molière. *Critique de "L'Ecole des Femmes"* (1663). Sc. vii.

Monro, D. H. *Argument of Laughter*. Victoria, Australia, 1951.

[Morris, Corbyn.] *An Essay towards Fixing the True Standards of Wit, Humour, Raillery, Satire, and Ridicule*. London, 1744.

Morris, Desmond. *The Naked Ape: A Zoologist's Study of the Human Animal*. New York, 1967.

Morrison, Jack. "A Note Concerning Investigations on the Constancy of Audience Laughter." *Sociometry*, 3 (1940), 179–85.

Muggeridge, Malcolm. "What's Funny about It?" *New York Times Book Review*, December 2, 1956.

Müller, Gottfried. *Theorie der Komik*. Würzburg, 1964.

Murphy, Brian, and Howard R. Pollio. "The Many Faces of Humor." *Psychological Record*, 25 (1975), 545–58.

Murray, Henry A., Jr. "The Psychology of Humor. 2. Mirth Responses to Disparagement Jokes as a Manifestation of an Aggressive Disposition." *Journal of Abnormal and Social Psychology*, 29 (1934), 66–81.

Nerhardt, Göran. "Humor and Inclination to Laugh: Emotional Reactions to Stimuli of Different Divergence from a Range of Expectancy." *Scandinavian Journal of Psychology*, 11 (1970), 185–95.

———. "Incongruity and Funniness: Towards a New Descriptive Model." In Chapman and Foot (1976), pp. 55–62.

Nicholi, Armand M., Jr., ed. *The Harvard Guide to Modern Psychiatry*. Cambridge, Mass., 1978.

Nicholson, Harold. *The English Sense of Humour and Other Essays*. London, 1956.

Nietzsche, Friedrich. *The Birth of Tragedy* (1872). Sec. vii.

O'Connell, Walter. "An Item Analysis of the Wit and Humor Appreciation Test." *Journal of Social Psychology*, 56 (1962), 271–76.

———. "Multidimensional Investigation of Freudian Humor." *Psychiatric Quarterly*, 38 (1964), 97–108.

Oliver, Edward James. *Hypocrisy and Humour*. New York, 1960.

Olson, Elder. *The Theory of Comedy*. Bloomington, Ind., 1968.

Pagnol, Marcel. *Notes sur le rire*. Paris, 1947.

Pascal, Blaise. *Pensées* (1662). Ed. H. F. Stewart. London, 1950. No. 109.

Paulos, John. *Mathematics and Humor*. Chicago, 1980.

Perl, Ruth Eastwood. "A Review of Experiments on Humor." *Psychological Bulletin*, 30 (1933), 752–63.

Piddington, Ralph. *The Psychology of Laughter*. London, 1933.

Pirandello, Luigi. *L'Umorismo* (1920). In *Saggi, poesie, scritti varii*, ed. Manlio Lo Vecchio Musti. Verona, 1960. P. 160.

Plato. *Philebus* (c. 360 B.C.). Trans. Benjamin Jowett. 48–49.

———. *Laws* (c. 340 B.C.). Trans. Benjamin Jowett. 7.816–17, 11.935–36.

———. *Republic* (c. 375 B.C.). Trans. Benjamin Jowett. III.395.

———. *Symposium* (c. 385 B.C.). Trans. Benjamin Jowett. 223.

Pollio, Howard. "What's So Funny?" *New Scientist*, 79 (1978), 774–77.

——— and John W. Edgerley. "Comedians and Comic Style." In Chapman and Foot (1976), pp. 236–41.

Potts, L. J. *Comedy*. London, 1948.

Priestley, Joseph. *A Course of Lectures on Oratory and Criticism*. London, 1777. Lecture 24.

Radcliffe-Brown, A. R. "On Joking Relationships." *Africa*, 13 (1940), 195–210.

———. "A Further Note on Joking Relationships." *Africa*, 19 (1949), 133–40.

———. *Structure and Function in Primitive Society*. Glencoe, Ill., 1952.

Rapp, Albert. "Toward an Eclectic and Multilateral Theory of Laughter and Humor." *Journal of General Psychology*, 36 (1947), 207–19.

———. *The Origins of Wit and Humor*. New York, 1951.

Rauleir, J. M. *Le rire et les exhilarants*. Paris, 1900.

Redlich, Frederick C., Jacob Levine, and Theodore P. Sohler. "A Mirth Response Test: Preliminary Report on a Psychodiagnostic Technique Utilizing Dynamics of Humor." *American Journal of Orthopsychiatry*, 21 (1951), 717–34.

Repplier, Agnes. *In Pursuit of Laughter*. Boston, 1936.

Ribot, Augustin Théodule. *La psychologie des sentiments*. Paris, 1902. Chap. 10.

Riccoboni, Antonio. *The Comic Art* (1585).

Richter, Johann Paul Friedrich [Jean-Paul]. *Vorschule der Aesthetik* (1803). Pt. 1, sec. 32.

Rigby, Peter. "Joking Relationships, Kin Categories, and Clanship among the Gogo." *Africa*, 28 (1968), 133–55.

Roberts, Allyn F., and Donald M. Johnson. "Some Factors Related to the Perception of Funniness in Humor Stimuli." *Journal of Social Psychology*, 46 (1957), 57–63.

Robortello, Francesco. *On Comedy* (1548).

Rothbart, Mary K. "Incongruity, Problem-Solving and Laughter." In Chapman and Foot (1976), pp. 37–52.

———. "Psychological Approaches to the Study of Humour." In Chapman and Foot (1978), pp. 87–94.

Saulnier, Claude. *Le sens du comique*. Paris, 1940.

Scheff, Thomas J. "A Theory of Catharsis in Drama" and "Humor and

Tension: The Effects of Comedy." In *Catharsis in Healing, Ritual, and Drama*. Berkeley, 1979. Chaps. 6 and 7.

Schlegel, August Wilhelm von. *Lectures on Dramatic Art and Literature* (1809). Trans. John Black, rev. A. J. W. Morrison. Lecture 13.

Schmidt, N. E., and D. I. Williams. "The Evolution of Theories of Humor." *Journal of Behavioral Science*, 1 (1971), 95–106.

Schoeller, Bernd. *Gelächter und Spannung; Studien zur Struktur des Heiteren Dramas*. Zurich, 1971.

Schopenhauer, Arthur. *The World as Will and Idea* (1818). Bk. 1, chap. 13.

Scott, Nathan A., Jr. "The Bias of Comedy and the Narrow Escape into Faith." *Christian Scholar*, 44 (1961), 9–39.

Seward, Samuel S., Jr. *The Paradox of the Ludicrous*. Stanford, Calif., 1930.

Shaftesbury, Anthony Ashley Cooper, 3d Earl of. *On the Freedom of Wit and Humour* (1711).

Shaw, George Bernard. "Meredith on Comedy." In *Our Theatres in the Nineties*. 3 vols. London, 1932. III, 86.

Shultz, Thomas R. "A Cognitive-Developmental Analysis of Humour." In Chapman and Foot (1976), pp. 11–36.

———. "A Cross-Cultural Study of the Structure of Humour." In Chapman and Foot (1978), pp. 175–79.

——— and F. Horibe. "Development of the Appreciation of Verbal Jokes." *Developmental Psychology*, 10 (1974), 13–20.

Sidis, Boris. *The Psychology of Laughter*. New York, 1919.

Skinner, B. F. *Verbal Behavior*. New York, 1957. Pp. 285–88.

Smith, Willard. *The Nature of Comedy*. Boston, 1930.

Spencer, Herbert. "The Physiology of Laughter." In *Essays, Scientific, Political and Speculative, 1868–1874*. Quoted in Nicolson, p. 12.

Spitz, René A. *The First Year of Life*. New York, 1965. Pp. 86–107 and *passim*.

Sroufe, L. Alan, and Jane Piccard Wunsch. "The Development of Laughter in the First Year of Life." *Child Development*, 43 (1972), 1326–44.

Stearns, Frederic R. *Laughing: Physiology, Pathophysiology, Psychology, Pathopsychology, and Development*. Springfield, Ill., 1972.

Stump, N. F. "Sense of Humor and Its Relationships to Personality, Scholastic Aptitude, Emotional Maturity, Height, and Weight." *Journal of General Psychology*, 20 (1939), 25–32.

Sully, James. *An Essay on Laughter*. London, 1902.

Suls, J. M. "A Two-Stage Model for the Appreciation of Jokes and Cartoons: An Information-Processing Analysis." In Goldstein and McGhee (1972), pp. 82–89.

Swabey, Marie Collins. *Comic Laughter: A Philosophical Essay*. New Haven, 1961.

Sypher, Wylie. "The Meanings of Comedy." In *Comedy*. Garden City, N.Y., 1956.

Tarachow, Sidney. "Remarks on the Comic Process and Beauty." *Psychoanalytic Quarterly*, 18 (1949), 215–26.

Thompson, William I. "Freedom and Comedy." *Tulane Drama Review*, 9 (1965), 216–30.

Thomson, George. *Aeschylus and Athens*. 2d ed. London, 1946.

Trachtenberg, Stanley. "The Economy of Comedy." *Psychoanalytic Review*, 62 (1975), 557–78.

Treadwell, Yvonne. "Bibliography of Empirical Studies of Wit and Humor." *Psychological Reports*, 20 (1967), 1079–83.

Trissino, Giovanni Georgio. *Poetics* (c. 1543–50). Division 6.

Turk, Edward Baron "Comedy and Psychoanalysis: The Verbal Component." *Philosophy and Rhetoric*, 12 (1979), 95–113.

Tynan, Kenneth. "Profile: Frolics and Detours of a Short Hebrew Man." *New Yorker*, October 30, 1978, pp. 46–130.

Tzetzes, John. *First Proem to Aristophanes* (c. 1110–80).

Updike, John. "From *Humor in Fiction*" (1970). In *Picked Up Pieces*. New York, 1975. Pp. 23–29.

Valentine, C. W. "La psychologie génétique du rire." *Journal de Psychologie Normale et Pathologique*, 33 (1936), 641–73.

Van Hooff, J. A. R. A. M. "A Comparative Approach to the Phylogeny of Laughter and Smiling." In *Non-Verbal Communication*, ed. R. A. Hinde. Cambridge, Eng., 1972.

Vischer, Friedrich Theodor. *Über das Erhabene und Komische*. Stuttgart, 1837.

Voltaire. *Dictionnaire philosophique*. Paris, 1764. S.v. *rire*.

Vos, Nelvin. *The Drama of Comedy: Victim and Victor*. Richmond, Va., 1966.

Wagoner, J. H., and C. B. Sullenberger. "Pupillary Size as an Indicator of Preference in Humor." *Perceptual & Motor Skills*, 47 (1978), 779–82.

Walpole, Horace. *Letter to Sir Horace Mann*. London, 1769.

Washburn, Ruth Wendell. "A Study of the Smiling and Laughing of Infants in the First Year of Life." *Genetic Psychology Monographs*, 5 (1929), 397–535.

Watts, Harold H. "The Sense of Regain: A Theory of Comedy." *University of Kansas City Review*, 13 (1946), 19–23.

Weisinger, Herbert. *Tragedy and the Paradox of the Fortunate Fall*. London, 1953.

Welsford, Enid. *The Fool*. London, 1945.

Whetstone, George. Dedication to *Promos and Cassandra* (1578). In *Elizabethan Critical Essays*, ed. Gregory Smith. London, 1904. Pp. 58–60.

White, R. W. "Ego and Reality in Psychoanalytic Theory." *Psychological Issues*, 3 (1963). Monograph 11.

Willeford, William. *The Fool and His Scepter: A Study in Clowns and Jesters and Their Audience*. Evanston, Ill., 1969.

Willmann, J. M. "An Analysis of Humor and Laughter." *American Journal of Psychology*, 53 (1940), 70–85.

Wilson, Katharine M. "The Sense of Humor." *Contemporary Review*, 131 (1927), 628–33.

Wolfenstein, Martha. *Children's Humor: A Psychological Analysis*. Glencoe, Ill., 1954.

Zillmann, Dolf, and Joanne R. Cantor. "A Disposition Theory of Humour and Mirth." In Chapman and Foot (1976), pp. 93–114.

Index

LAUGHING

Designed by G. T. Whipple, Jr.
Composed by Eastern Graphics
in 10 point Linotron 202 Palatino, 3 points leaded,
with display lines in Palatino.
Printed offset by Thomson-Shore, Inc.
on Warren's Number 66 text, 50 pound basis.
Bound by John H. Dekker & Sons
in Holliston book cloth
and stamped in Kurz-Hastings foil.

Library of Congress Cataloging in Publication Data

HOLLAND, NORMAN NORWOOD, 1927–
    Laughing, a psychology of humor.

    Bibliography: p.
    Includes index.
    1. Laughter.   2. Wit and humor—Psychological
aspects.   I. Title.
BF575.L3H64   808.7'01   82-7458
ISBN 0-8014-1449-0   AACR2